Plants and Animals i
Life of the Kuna

DATE DUE

OCT 1 3 1998	
JAN 2 6 1999	
JAN 2 1 2003	
Capilano	
due Apr 3/04	

BRODART   Cat. No. 23-221

iLAS Translations from Latin America Series

**Institute of Latin American Studies
University of Texas at Austin**

Plants and Animals in the Life of the Kuna

by
Jorge Ventocilla
Heraclio Herrera
Valerio Núñez

Edited by Hans Roeder
Translated by Elisabeth King

University of Texas Press, Austin

First Edition, 1995

Requests for permission to reproduce material from this work should be sent to
Permissions, University of Texas Press, P.O. Box 7819, Austin, Texas 78713-
7819

♾ The paper used in this publication meets the minimum requirements of
American National Standard for Information Sciences—Permanence of Paper
for Printed Library Materials, ANSI Z39.48–1984.

Library of Congress Cataloging-in-Publication Data

Ventocilla, Jorge, 1955–
    [Plantas y animales en la vida del pueblo Kuna. English]
    Plants and animals in the life of the Kuna / by Jorge Ventocilla, Heraclio
Herrera, Valerio Núñez ; edited by Hans Roeder ; translated by Elisabeth
King.
        p.   cm. — (Translations from Latin America Series)
    Includes bibliographical references and index.
    ISBN 0-292-78725-1 (cloth : alk. paper). — ISBN 0-292-78726-X (paper :
alk. paper)
    1. Cuna Indians—Ethnobiology. 2. Environmental protection—Panama.
3. Ethnobiology—Panama. I. Herrera, Heraclio. II. Núñez, Valerio,
1956– . III. Roeder, Hans. IV. Title. V. Series.
F1565.2.C8V4613 1995   95-2942
333.9513' 097287—dc20   CIP

Contents

Figures

Tables

Maps

Foreword

The Kuna of Panama have been learning the same hard environmental lesson as the rest of the world, that one must protect nature against oneself as well as against others.

Against external challenges and threats the Kuna have enjoyed remarkable success. Early in this century, they were menaced by intrusive rubber tappers, turtlers, and gatherers of ivory nuts; by manganese mines and two large banana plantations; by a government-sponsored colony; and by an official program to subdue the indigenous population and suppress its culture.

Provoked into a brief rebellion in 1925, the Kuna regained most of what they had lost through a happy combination of courage, organization, and good luck. They expelled the intruders, reincorporated the banana plantations as they succumbed to blight, and negotiated territorial guarantees and a modus vivendi with the national government. In 1938 Kuna territory was incorporated as the Comarca de San Blas, today known as Kuna Yala.

In recent years, new intruders have encroached on Kuna lands. From the West and the South, landless mestizo peasants have been sweeping across the Darién region, cutting down the forest and converting it to pasture. When the Kuna first awoke to the danger presented by this hungry pastoral army, the advance guard, coming over the mountains into Kuna Yala, had already stolen a march on them. In the East, impoverished black Colombians have also penetrated Kuna defenses, crossing the border to pan for gold and colonize Kuna land. This time the Kuna mobilized nonviolently. During the 1980s, teams of volunteers demarcated the borders of Kuna Yala, and through the PEMASKY Project, an effort financed by international agencies but initiated and run by the Kuna themselves, they worked to turn the mountainous boundary lands into a forest reserve.

The campaign against these external threats has not ended. In the course of the struggle, however, as the Kuna have taken stock of the natural environment and their place in it, they have increasingly lamented losses and dangers that cannot be blamed on invading peasants: lobsters have disappeared from the daily diet; fishermen no longer find the huge schools of tiny fish used as bait; few sea turtles lay their eggs; game retreats into the mountains; blights destroy coconut palms; and farmland grows scarce.

As many Kuna see it, the problems come in part through loss of knowledge, the intimate knowledge of forest and marine environments retained by the oldest hunters, fishermen, agriculturists, and, especially, medicinal curers. As many young Kuna abandon traditional subsistence for paid labor, either in Kuna Yala or in the city, and as almost no one under thirty seriously apprentices to learn traditional medicine, the store of environmental knowledge rapidly diminishes and, with it, the intimacy of the Kuna's connection with the natural world.

This volume, the work of two Kuna biologists and a Panamanian colleague, confronts the environmental crisis in Kuna Yala by warning of the dangers at hand and by attempting to rebuild a connection with the natural world through a combination of traditional and scientific knowledge. For readers, non-Kuna as well as Kuna, it offers information otherwise unavailable on Isthmian human ecology—on hunting practices, agriculture, the medicinal use of plants, and even the commoditization of traditional forest products. Paradoxically, non-Kuna readers will gain something extra from this book precisely because they are *not* its primary audience. Because the authors are speaking most of all to their own people, the text allows the rest of us to eavesdrop, to listen as they exhort each other to wake up and to change.

The authors locate many of Kuna Yala's troubles in the market economy, in a perverse alliance between insiders and outsiders that makes cash-hungry Kuna the agents of foreign economic interests. While this criticism is well placed, there are other factors at play, and the predicament into which the Kuna have fallen is complex and extremely difficult to deal with. Also at work are population growth, careless practices, subsistence pressure, and other nonmarket sources of environmental degradation. And one should not underplay the Kuna's long involvement in the world economy—men may dive for lobsters less out of greed or boredom with traditional agriculture than to compensate for a declining trade in coconuts and a shrinking job market. The Kuna, like the indigenous peoples of North America who enthusiastically killed beaver so that Europeans could wear tall hats, have been drawn into a system vastly larger and more powerful than their own society. If they are to survive as a people into the next century, they must reconcile the subsistence and market economies as well as protect the borders of their small enclave.

Ever since the Enlightenment, sympathetic Europeans and Euro-Americans have looked to indigenous peoples, to Natural Man, for environmental wisdom. What the Kuna can teach us in this volume is that there are no easy solutions or innate ecologists, that even a people who see themselves placed on Mother Earth to care for her creation must confront the harm they do her. The struggle, it turns out, encompasses and implicates us all.

—James Howe
Massachusetts Institute of Technology

Acknowledgments

With this text we hope to return to the Kuna cultural information that is rightfully theirs, information that we often obtained by direct communication with the Kuna themselves. Nevertheless, we assume complete responsibility for the claims we make here. We would also appreciate any comments.

There are many people to whom we would like to express our gratitude. Without their help, this book would have been difficult to make a reality. First, we would like to thank the people from the Kuna communites who helped us in many ways, whether by offering us a glass of *inna*, transporting us in a dugout, or lending us a hammock for the night.

Many Kuna leaders and experts supported our research: Cacique General Leonidas Kantule Valdez, *saila* Demóstenes Valdez (from Gangandi), *nele* Roberto Pérez (Gangandi), *argar* Rafael Harris (Miria Ubigandup), *inaduled* Inaiduli Osvaldo López (Miria Ubigandup), *inaduled* Gabriel Mojica (Ukupseni), *argar dummad* Gilberto Arias (Mandi Ubigandup), *saila* Antonio Alfaro (Nusadup), *saila* Robin Vásquez (Guebdi), *sailagan* Rodrigo Stocel and Ebelardo Brenes (Ukupseni), and *saila* Abelardo González (Dubuala).

Various people collaborated with us in the field, especially Rutilio Paredes (Usdup), Avelino and Deyanira Pérez (Gardi Sugdup), Johnny Morris, Lucio Arosemena, Gricelio Grimaldo, Wellis Muñoz (Ukupseni), Belisario Porras and Pedro Calderón (Dubuala).

The first draft of the book was reviewed by Hans Roeder, James Howe, and Arysteides Turpana. We thank them for their patience and improvement of material that at the beginning was quite raw. The final draft was critiqued by Mac Chapin, Joel Sherzer, Nicanor González, Reuter Orán, Ramón Oviero, Georgina De Alba, Adalberto Padilla, and, again, by Arysteides Turpana and James Howe. Other people critiqued sections of the manuscript: Rutilio Paredes, Jesús Alemancia, Rodolfo Herrera, Beatriz and Eligio Alvarado, Gubiler Castillo, Gabriel Jácome, Elena

Lombardo, Arcadio Castillo, and Francisco Herrera. We thank Olaidi for the information about the overexploitation of the lobster and Katherine Orr for information about its biology.

The World Wildlife Fund (WWF), through its Central American Regional Office, supplied the necessary funds for the production and printing of the Spanish version of the book. We are especially grateful to Miguel Cifuentes and Oscar Brenes of the WWF for their faith in our project.

The Spanish version of the book was printed in the graphics workshop of the National Institute of Panamanian Culture (INAC). We appreciate the support of the director, Dr. Alberto Osorio, and of Professor Ramón Oviero, head of Editorial Mariano Arosemena.

The Smithsonian Tropical Research Institute (STRI) Office of Education and Conservation offered support in many ways, especially logistical help. We would like to direct our particular thanks to Dr. Ira Rubinoff, STRI's director.

Initially, the Fundación de Parques Nacionales y Medio Ambiente (Fundación Panamá) and, later, the Fundación Dobbo Yala administered the project that resulted in this book. For several years the authors have been supported in many ways by the Proyecto de Estudios para el Manejo de las Areas Silvestres de Kuna Yala (PEMASKY).

Jorge Ventocilla's research on hunting and subsistence practices in Gangandi was supported by STRI, WWF, PEMASKY, the Programa Regional para Manejo de Vida Silvestre en Mesoamérica y el Caribe (Universidad Nacional de Heredia, Costa Rica), the U.S. Fish and Wildlife Service, and the German Service for Academic Interchange (DAAD).

Conservation International, the International Union for the Conservation of Nature (IUCN), and the New York Botanical Garden, financed Heraclio Herrera's *ueruk* palm project.

Kuna artists Ologuagdi and Enrique Tejada created the illustrations. These illustrations are based on photos taken by the authors as well as by Olonigdi, Rutilio Paredes, Carl Hansen, Andy Young, and Nicholas Smythe. We appreciate the help of Ologuagdi and Gubiler Castillo in the preparation of the maps. These maps are lovingly dedicated to the students of Kuna Yala so that they can learn the names of their rivers and mountains.

Kuna experts, leaders, and community members offered their opinions on questions about the environment, the significance of the fifth centenary, and the future of Kuna Yala as part of a survey conducted by Valerio Núñez. Space limitations allow us to include only four of these interviews, although we spoke with some twenty people. Prof. Reuter Orán from Dad Nakue Dupbir helped translate the taped testimonies.

Special thanks to our editor, Hans Roeder, whose direction and particular interest in this book were essential in making it what it is.

Our friends and families inspired us with enthusiasm and their questions about how we were doing and when this book would finally appear.

Here you have the work of many hands, which represents many hours of labor and a great deal of patience and care.

Plants and Animals in the
Life of the Kuna

1

Baba's Creation

The earth is the mother of all things, the Great Mother. She is the guardian who caringly watches over all that exists. She has *burba* and we live on her.

The Great Mother helps us stay in equilibrium. Our fathers teach us that the world has eight spiritual levels, where one finds gold, silver, iron, and many other minerals that sustain Mother Earth. If we allow all of this to be exploited, the trees will die and production will dwindle. Therefore, we have to take care of them, not abuse them.

Our body is the same. We, too, have iron and gold in us. Once you break an arm or a leg, you will never be able to move it as you once did. Remember that your body and Mother Earth are similar. They are the creation of Bab Dummad, Great Father, whom we also call Baba. He and his wife, Nan Dummad, Great Mother, created all that exists.

The rain passes over, just as clouds and winds do. They are attracted by the trees that refresh the environment. Thus, trees are indispensable and we cannot mistreat them. Trees are not here by chance. Their roots penetrate the earth through the sixth level and they emerge onto the surface as well. Trees renew their sap by drinking river water through their roots. Water circulates through all of their branches and leaves.

Trees have sap, resin, and who do you think drinks the sap? Mother Earth. That is how she strengthens herself.

The earth is covered with trees of all kinds, which give it life and strength. This is Baba's creation. Thus, our fathers tell us: "You have to learn all of this to truly love Mother Earth."

The thick cords, like ropes, that you see hanging from the trees are medicinal vines that serve as perches for birds that come to enjoy the surroundings and the trees. Trees never harm us. They protect us and provide medicines to treat our ills.

Trees give their fruit to feed the animals. They don't bear fruit needlessly. If trees didn't produce so abundantly, there would be no collared or white-lipped peccaries, no birds. Therefore, we must take care: trees are our life; they feed us and protect us.

Figure 1. Cacique General Enrique Guerrero. (Ologuagdi)

All of this is essential. If, by chance, the breezes don't blow, the mists won't fall. Many times a torrential rain falls, and after a while the sun shines again. The sun is also necessary; our life depends on it.

Nan Gabsus,[1] Mother of the Night who cares for the children, the darkness, is essential as well. We sleep and, at the appointed time, Mother Earth awakens us.

Our prophet Ibeler, or Dad Ibe, who was transformed into the sun, wakes us and invites us to work. Ibeler gave us all of our songs and traditions. Everything that we do is not our own doing; someone urges us to do it.

Ibeler loved nature. He cared for them all: the smallest insects, like the fire ants, the scorpions, the spiders, the vipers. He could not bear to see floating branches, which he rescued and put in a place where they could grow.

The jungle where the wild animals live—the snake, the puma, the jaguar—rarely frightens us when we go into her interior because Ibeler guides and protects us.

Olodualigipileler, the moon, father of Ibeler, is also important to us. He notes our ages. When I see a small child I ask: "How many moons does this child have?"

The elements of nature are not here in vain. Each has its function. When a hard rain falls, it is to let us rest. But even more, it is to clean the natural world, which gets dirty during the summer. Thus, the rivers overflow their banks, removing the debris that has fallen in during the dry season.

Our forefathers lived on the mainland along the banks of the great rivers in the mountains before they came to know the sea. The rivers were places that they chose for their dwelling places. Our fathers were strong because they were nourished by the plants and trees that surrounded them.

The rivers that they cared for so much were full of stones and had strong currents. Our fathers drank from these rivers, so they were strong and they understood the natural world well. The rivers touch the roots of many medicinal plants and therefore we have *akwanusagana*. This is why the old people then were much stronger than the men who live on the islands today.

The elders also knew of the existence of four continents and that one day white people would arrive in Abya Yala,[2] as we call the American continent. All of this was prophesied by the *nelegan*, our traditional doctors, who see by means of dreams. In their dreams our fathers saw tall bearded men.

The Spanish sacked our towns and killed our wise grandmothers, who wove hammocks and made marvelous things with clay. Our grandmothers made necklaces. The Spanish came to claim the gold in our rivers. They also killed the great specialists in botany and sacred song.

We know, as our fathers have told us, that there would be those who would offer us money and promises in exchange for the resources that we have in our territory. So that we would not be fooled, the *caciques* Simral Colman and Nele Kantule, among others, created schools. The first school was created in 1907 by Gasso, the priest. And in 1931 a little school of three grades was opened in Usdup, a result of the Dule Revolution. Before, the *uagmala* (outsiders), called us brute Indians and savages. Now they respect us, and they know that we are as well educated as they are.

We look upon Panama as our father. But the Government does not help us with anything that happens in our territory, which has been invaded by colonists.

We supported the Government with our vote, and now that the elections approach, they say that they consult us, but they have not respected our demands. Thus it is said of us: When will they ever learn? How long will they continue to allow themselves to be deceived? But we will continue to advance. We can rely on people who are well-trained university graduates. We are not going to act as we have before. Our decisions will be firm.

When work on the road to Gardi began, I was in Udirbi, where the road to El Llano enters our territory.[3] I expressed my interest in the conservation of our forests as well as my wariness of transnationals who come to offer us their dollars; they become millionaires while we remain poor.

Unlike them, none of us are millionaires. We work the earth. This is our tradition and our culture.

Let us talk about lobsters and iguanas. Our fathers did not sell lobsters. And the iguanas were abundant in the *suu*. One could find them in great numbers.

Our fathers did not use the hunting weapons that are used today. Moreover, they hunted only to survive.

If we begin to hunt indiscriminately, we will put an end to lobsters and iguanas. We know this from warnings that our fathers, who were well informed about these subjects, left for us. The same thing is happening to the turtles. We ought to let them reproduce. We cannot collect all of the eggs that they lay on the beaches. We would like to regulate the sale of lobster but we have not been able to restrain the buyers. Our General Congress has made statements to this effect. It is not true that the *caciques* are not doing anything. The Government is familiar with the problem and has acted in our favor, but beyond that, nothing happens.

In essence, the sea is like a forest populated with different plants and animals. We should take care of our natural resources. A group of Mexican Indians who visited us impressed this on us. We should be aware of what is happening at this moment in the mines of Río Pito, near the Colombian border, where Chocó and Colombians are in the process of extracting gold illegally.

❖ ❖

In 1925, Simral Colman and Nele Kantule launched the Revolution. Why? They did it to oppose the abuses of the colonial police. Nele Kantule said:

> Bab Dummad gave us culture. So that my culture is not lost and so that we recognize ourselves as the Olodulegan, our sisters must continue to wear their molas, their gold nose rings, their earrings and gold breastplates.
>
> I am happy that we have *gandurgan* and that there is communal labor in the construction of houses and canoes. This is how we establish our worth, the feeling that we are brothers and sisters and that we have a culture. If we start to lose our culture, we will be going down another road, right away things won't be as they were, and everyone will think in terms of money. This is why I established the school, to defend our culture.

This is how Colman and Iguanibiginya spoke.

Now our grandmothers and grandfathers have gone to Panama, and I don't know what they are doing there. They didn't need to go. Already, they don't think about coming back; already they have made the city their home. They have forgotten their culture.

No one is here forever.

I know that I'm going to die.

I would like to leave all that I know to the new generation.

I want to leave ideas so that everyone can benefit from them. This way they will remember me forever as an individual who dedicated himself to planting mangoes, cacao, and coconuts. He dies, but his plants remain for the good of his children.

This text represents the thoughts of the Kuna cacique Enrique Guerrero (1912–1992), recorded by Valerio Núñez in the community of Ogobsukun in April 1992. The cacique died two months later.

Notes

1. "'Mother sleep-brought'," another manifestation of Great Mother.
2. A ceremonial name for the Kuna homeland or the Americas as a whole.
3. The El Llano–Gardí road is the only road into Kuna Yala. It was built in the early 1970s and connects the Pan American Highway to the Caribbean coast.

2

Ready to Change?

For a number of years, we have been developing environmental education programs in Kuna Yala. There has been a great deal of discussion about the principle of saving traditional ecological knowledge and about how to "return" it to the community.

We began with several projects. We have held workshops with schoolteachers and have encouraged the revival of traditional technologies (such as reforestation in Ukupseni with the *ueruk* palm). Now we are beginning to work directly with children, because we believe that environmental education should be part of their training from the beginning. In the Children's Art Workshop in the community of Gardi Sugdup, we are working to rescue ecological and cultural ideas via painting, theater, poetry, and other art forms as practiced by children. Through trial and error, we have provided continuity for the evolution of environmental education in Kuna Yala.

Thus, we are extremely pleased with this book. In its Spanish-language version it is primarily intended for the Kuna public: for Kuna grade school and university students and their teachers, both those who live within Kuna Yala and those who live outside the Comarca. We also hope that the translation will allow a non-Kuna audience to become interested.

We have made an effort to write in clear and accessible language, to overcome the limitations of scientific discourse while insisting on the accuracy of the information and the indispensable rigor of a text that treats the people, the flora, and the fauna of Kuna Yala.

The book is a guide to the physical space in which the majority of the Kuna live. By physical space we mean the tangible environment that surrounds all living things, including human beings.

As environmental educators, we are aware that no one loves what she or he has not learned to understand, that one has to want to protect the environment. To want to protect the environment, one must first understand what needs to be protected. To this end, the book gives, for example, the names and locations of the principal rivers and mountains of Kuna Yala, including the first published maps to integrate this information. It also describes physical characteristics of the sea as a natural resource because it is from the sea that the Kuna people obtain much of their nutritional and material livelihood. In addition, the book contains a wealth of descriptive information and illustrations of the flora and fauna of Kuna territory—the land that forms the basis of the Kuna's lives, their traditions, and their culture.

The other focus of the book is the interpretation of Kuna knowledge and Kuna cultural practices in the context of their environment and illustrated by a discussion of subsistence methods in several communities. The structure of their subsistence economy lets the Kuna use the resources necessary for their "sustainable" method of survival. But unfortunately, as we will demonstrate, the Kuna themselves are eroding the base of their sustainable way of life.

What is subsistence? Bernard Nietschmann, a geographer who has studied the Miskito on the Caribbean coast of Nicaragua, puts it well: "The very word 'subsistence' conjures up images of a hard, marginal life, continuous work just to survive, inability to produce surplus, low return from labor, little security of life, poor diet and nutrition, and a universal level of livelihood which is an impediment to economic development." But when one tries to understand the economies of societies considered to be "primitive," first one has to remember that "there are two roads to affluence, by either satisfying wants through producing much, or by desiring little. The assumption in our economic system is that man's wants are great and his means are limited. For many primitive peoples, however, wants are limited and means are great."[1]

We have been very interested in the consideration of subsistence; it is a basic theme that ought to be included more often in the discussion of the environment. A discussion of subsistence leads us to ask ourselves four fundamental questions:

1. What are our real needs?
2. What do we need to satisfy them?
3. Is it possible to reconcile the voracity of societies that have market economies and the availability of natural resources?
4. What kind of society is sustainable?

These are difficult times of transition for indigenous cultures whose lives are intimately linked to the tropical forest. In the case of the Kuna, the problem is exacerbated by colonists who have already arrived in their territory and who are destroying the forest and the land that in one way or another have traditionally been the Kuna's birthright. This intrusion weakens the basis of their survival as an ethnic group within Panama's multicultural and multiethnic state. Indigenous people have always experienced encounters with Western cultures and economies as violent shocks from which they emerge extremely battered.

The calls of indigenous peoples for the maintenance of their territorial boundaries must be heard. Indigenous people need their territory to subsist, that is to say, to survive.

If we admit that societal changes are inevitable, and moreover, that our culture is no longer sustainable, then we had better prepare to change.

The voices that we hear in the pages of this book are, for the most part, Kuna. They are voices that, like the four interviews, represent the wisdom and the material and spiritual impetus that can motivate us to make the necessary change.

There are innumerable signals that indicate that we have very little time left to accomplish an urgent necessity. Are we ready to change?

—Jorge Ventocilla

Note

1. Nietschmann, "The Substance of Subsistence," p. 167.

3

The Kuna

It is estimated that when the Europeans arrived in the New World, approximately 57 million people were living on this continent. Of these, 5 to 6 million inhabited Central America. A century and a half later, after the European invasion, Central America's population was drastically reduced.

After five hundred years, forty-five indigenous cultures still survive in Central America, with an estimated total population of five million. Only Guatemala and Belize have a proportionately larger indigenous population than does Panama. Several native communities in Panama are considered to be the least acculturated in the region.

According to the 1990 census, Panama had an indigenous population of at least 225,373 in six groups: Guaymí, Kuna, Emberá, Bokota, Wounaan, and Teribe (map 1). The Ngobe (or Guaymí), with a population of 123,000, are the most numerous. One in every ten Panamanians, then, belongs to an indigenous group.

The Kuna people are the best-known ethnic group both within and outside of Panama. They collectively hold the Comarca Kuna Yala (the District of Kuna Yala, also known as San Blas): 320,600 hectares on the mainland plus the adjacent waters. Kuna Yala extends from northeastern to southeastern Panama, from Punta San Blas (79° west) to Puerto Obaldía, near the Colombian border (77° west) (map 2). Kuna Yala is approximately 226 kilometers (140 miles) long.

The census taken by the Ministry of Health in 1989 indicates that at least 40,864 persons live in the Comarca. The great majority of the Kuna live on forty islands. Eleven communities, however, are located on the coast itself—in parts of the littoral that lack islands, and two (Gangandi and Mandi) are situated a few kilometers inland. According to the 1990 national census, the total Kuna population of Panama was 47,298, though, for those familiar with the census figures as they apply to the indigenous populations, they are approximations and lower than the actual population.

In Kuna Yala, communities are strategically situated near the coast, where agricultural areas and vital natural resources such as water, firewood, and construction materials are easily accessible. Some 3,000 other Kuna inhabit the Pacific slope of Panama in the watersheds of the Bayano, Chucunaque, and Tuira rivers. They live in a different environment and are considered to be remnants of the ancient Kuna migration from the Pacific to the Caribbean. A few thousand Kuna live in northern Colombia. From a cultural standpoint, the three groups of Kuna do not differ greatly and they recognize each other as members of a single ethnic group.

For years there has been migration out of the Comarca, but today it is becoming more pronounced. It is estimated that up to 30 percent of the Kuna population lives outside of their original homeland, either in Panama City and Colón or on the banana plantations of Changuinola (see map 1).

Kuna communities are composed, in considerable part, of children and young people, as is the case in all of Latin America.

The debate about whether the indigenous peoples that Spanish chroniclers met in the Darién in the beginning of the sixteenth century were ancestors of the Kuna is still unresolved. One school of thought maintains that the Kuna are their direct descendants—regardless of cultural and linguistic differences. Another claims that the Kuna emigrated from Colombia after the sixteenth century. Ethnolinguistic evidence strongly supports the theory of a Kuna origin to the west of Panama, even that the Kuna might have migrated into present-day Colombia and later returned to the territories in Panama that they occupy today.

According to oral tradition, the Dule (Kuna) people originated in the Sierra Nevada de Santa Marta in northern Colombia. One of the most notable experts in Kuna culture, the late *saila* Horacio Méndez, agrees that the Kuna originally came from five areas in the Sierra Nevada, and that, because of pressure from neighboring tribes, they were forced to immigrate to the plains of Amukadiuar (the present-day Atrato River). Much later, persecution by other indigenous groups and the flooding of the Atrato River drove them to take refuge in the mountains of the Darién, in particular on Mount Tacarcuna (at 1,875 meters, the highest mountain in eastern Panama). Even today, it is a sacred place for the Dule people.

About their time in the lands of the Darién, we are told of Duiren, a *nele* who taught the group how to defend itself. The Tuira River takes its name from Duiren (which some traditional teachers believe is a nickname for Olonekikinya). In stories about this epoch, the *sailagan* speak of dispersed groups of Kuna, rather than of a single entity. In the Congress

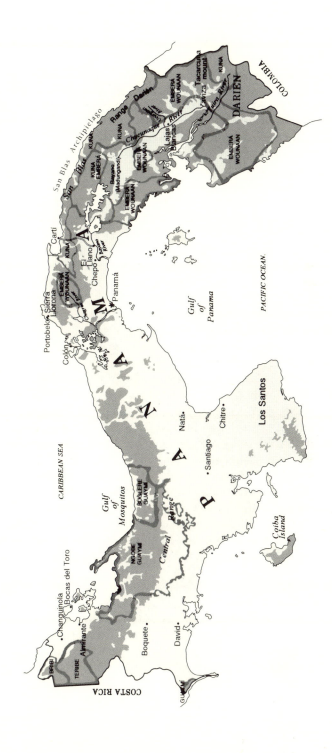

Map 1. Panama's Six Indigenous Groups

house, the *onmakednega*, the meeting place in each Kuna community, the elders say: "We are not from this little islet. We are from the great rivers. Enemy forces imprisoned us and forced us to emigrate. Our lands are there, across the frontier."

In the last few centuries the Dule have been displaced toward the Caribbean, and it is only relatively recently that they established themselves on the islands that they inhabit today. For many years, they visited these coasts but the gradual movement of the population to the islands started only in the middle of the nineteenth century.

James Howe, who has worked for years in Kuna Yala, refers in the following terms to the theme of the origins and dispersion of the Kuna people:

> No matter where they came from, the Kuna have lived for centuries in the Darién and the Golfo de Urabá. The theories of the origin of the Kuna as an ethnic group lack sound evidence; nevertheless, we know that in the era of Balboa there were already people speaking Kuna in Urabá and in the Darién, because they were using the word *oba* for corn and *ulu* for canoe. Moreover, we know very well that in the colonial epoch there were Kuna in almost all parts of the Darién because the geographic names are Kuna, even in areas where today there are no Kuna. On the maps I do not see places without Kuna names, with the exception of some streams near the coast in the region of Chimán, and on the Pacific coast near Colombia. The first big river that does not have a Kuna name is the Sambú. One may use the same rationale to argue that the Kuna have lived in San Blas for centuries. In the times of Balboa there were indigenous people on the Caribbean coast, but because of the presence of pirates, no one would live there because there were no defensible sites. Nevertheless, colonial sources say that there were indigenous people on both sides of the mountains. Maps from the 18th Century show that there were Kuna living not far from the coast, exploiting coastal resources but living in more defensible places, a bit upriver. In brief, life on the islands is new for the Kuna, but their presence in San Blas is not.[1]

It is important to remember that the Dule people have been associated with environments on the mainland and thus their cultural heritage is terrestrial, in forested environments along rivers. Nevertheless, many aspects of Kuna culture are closely connected with the coastal environment. There are strong sentimental roots to Kuna Yala, and the Kuna often speak with feeling about *yar suit*, the "long land."

Since the arrival of the Europeans, the Dule people have maintained partial geographic isolation with respect to foreign societies. By managing their contact with other societies, they have succeeded in maintaining a degree of political and cultural autonomy that is exceptional among the indigenous peoples of the Americas today. Through trial and error, they have adapted to the radical changes of Latin America in the twentieth century and have preserved a good part of their cultural identity and unity.

Another famous characteristic of the Dule is the production of the mola, the blouse panels used by women in their traditional dress and sold as crafts. Molas still symbolize the identity of the Kuna people to outsiders, and their designs may be very elaborate.

However, to the Kuna themselves, it is the songs and stories that are part of the meetings of the community congress that maintain the essential themes of the culture and that reveal its basic religious and moral character.

It is also quite common that intrinsic characteristics that define an indigenous group are overlooked. For example, the Dule traditionally maintain, sponsor, and celebrate the solidarity and unity of their communities. There are still communities in which barter of food and assistance strongly binds individuals and groups. As an anthropologist who worked with them remarks, the Kuna "talk about their generosity constantly" and the absence of exchange "marks the limits of their social world."

But these practices have begun to diminish as relationships become oriented more toward money than toward solidarity. In this continuing process, the logic, if we can call it that, of the consumer society puts pressure on the Kuna lifestyle and the way the Kuna relate to each other and modifies that lifestyle.

The Kuna Way of Life

Agriculture
The Kuna are primarily farmers and fishers. They practice slash-and-burn agriculture and obtain much of their protein from ocean fish. Hunting and the gathering of forest products are secondary.

The Kuna way of life is definitely conditioned by their location on islands along the coast. Their subsistence requires almost daily visits to agricultural plots. They must travel from homes on the islands to their farms (*nainumar*) on the mainland. The canoe trip alone, from the ocean to the farm, may take several hours (fig. 3). If they are working far inland, they may construct a shelter in which to spend the night. In Kuna Yala there are a few burros and mules only in the communities near the Colombian border and in Mandi, areas where campesinos live nearby.

Figure 2. Kuna woman in traditional dress, working on a mola. (Ologuagdi)

The Kuna farm along a coastal strip that can extend several kilometers inland. The land that is worked is concentrated along rivers or near the coast, which facilitates the transport of agricultural products to island communities. Agriculture is better characterized as extensive rather than intensive, with *masi* (bananas or plaintains) as the principal product. Besides *masi*, *oba* (corn), *mama* (yucca), *oros* (rice), *oros ginnid*

Figure 3. A group of Kuna men carrying a recently made dugout canoe out of the forest. (Ologuagdi)

(red rice), *gay* (sugarcane), and various other edible plants, both domesticated and wild, are among the primary plants the Kuna use. On a *nainu* one may find many useful species, from fruit trees to edible plants to plants used to extract dyes for traditional ceremonies and cosmetics.

The Kuna intercrop, sometimes among trees. The agricultural cycle generally begins when trees are cleared during December and January.

Primary forest is cleared first; younger vegetation is left until March and April. This activity is considered hard labor and diverts attention from other activities such as fishing (which is difficult during this season because of strong dry season winds).

In general, the period from December through April (the dry season) can be characterized as a period of scarcity. Burning off begins in March and planting follows a few days or weeks later, after the first rains, in April or May. In some parts of the Comarca it is customary for the Kuna to plant a second crop in October or November, and in scarce and highly fertile lands along the banks of the largest rivers they plant in November and December, a practice called *yolep*.

Two elements distinguish agriculture as practiced in Kuna Yala from agriculture as practiced by campesinos on the Pacific slope. The primary difference is that there is no cattle ranching in the Comarca and no pastureland: farmland is fallow from four to ten years before successive cultivation for a two- to three-year period. In the Pacific sector, such an agricultural cycle is impractical because cattle ranching ensures that recently logged forest will end up as permanent pastureland within a few years.

The second important difference is that the Asian grasses *Saccharum spontaneum* and *Hyparrhenia rufa*, common elsewhere in Panama, have not reached Kuna Yala. These grasses impede natural regeneration of secondary forest once they become established in a logged area. Therefore, extensive areas become useless, as not even cattle can feed on these plants.

The land of the Comarca is, then, primarily an expanse of tropical jungle that runs down from the Cordillera de San Blas to the Carribean coast, an abrupt topograpical change. A narrow strip of relatively flat land follows jungle that drops abruptly from the San Blas range toward the Caribbean, where the land flattens into a narrow coastal plain. Agricultural areas in the lowlands are mixed plots of crop plants, vegetation in different stages of regeneration, and primary forest. Closer to the sea, the countryside is covered with coconut groves and mangrove swamps.

In general, people distinguish between the *neg serred* ("old place," or primary forest) and the *neg nuchukua* ("young place," or secondary forest, known also as *nainu serred*, "old farmland"). *Nainu* is the name given to small farms or cultivated plots. Inhabitants also use local names; for example, in Gangandi the people refer to the *mergi serred*, which grows in sites that were formerly banana plantations (established in this area in the 1920s).[2]

It is uncommon for the Kuna to use measures of land area. When primary forest is first cleared, rivers, streams, and mountain ridges are used to demarcate agricultural plots. When the owner divides the land—for example to pass it on to children—fruit trees are planted to serve as the future boundary lines of the *nainumar.*

Land Tenure and Inheritance

There are five classes of land tenure: land as private property, family holdings, communal land, land belonging to associations or groups, and borrowed land. The land becomes someone's property when that person cuts primary forest. Sometimes it is cut by groups, or *sociedades*, which become the original owners. The children of members may then inherit the rights associated with land ownership. Land may also be worked by communal labor, but it is more common for the forests to be cut by individual men; thus the initial owner is usually a man.

The land is inherited by both sons and daughters and the right to work it may be bought and sold, but only by Dule, because by law no non-Dule may own property in Kuna Yala. Some land, especially in secondary growth, may be inherited by brothers and sisters and remain undivided for years. In some regions, family coconut groves are harvested on a rotating basis by the members of a family group who share the land rights. Because land may be inherited by women, many women own numerous tracts of land, a fact that is extremely important in Kuna social structure.

Sources of Income

The *ogob* trade with Colombian traders has been the principal source of income for years. In the nineteenth century many coconut groves had already been planted in the Comarca. In 1967, the commercialization of coconuts represented 70 percent of total income. This activity has resulted in the conversion of some islands and extensive coastal zones into coconut monocultures. On the other hand, Colombian trading boats bring products to sell on the islands like oil, salt, gasoline, hammocks, dugout canoes, coffee, rubber boots, and sugar—indispensable products for everyday living.

Subsistence labor continues to be the principal occupation of the majority of the population, but the sale of lobsters, tortoiseshell, and molas, salaried work on the islands, and tourism, have greatly expanded in the last twenty to thirty years, and indeed some of these activities have become part of the Kuna way of life since the last century. For a long time, the Kuna have been producing for a market outside of the Comarca. Their subsistence depends completely on tools and products that they do not make themselves.

The employment of Kuna who emigrate from Kuna Yala to the urban centers of Panama City, Colón, and the banana plantations of Changuinola is, after the sale of coconuts, the primary source of income.

—Jorge Ventocilla

Notes

1. James Howe, personal communication with the author.
2. The Kuna call people from the United States and people who look like them *mergi*.

4

Rivers and Mountains

The Comarca of Kuna Yala is located in the central portion of the geological formation known as the Arco Oriental del Norte, which extends from the Sierra Llorona in Portobelo to the Tacarcuna range. Beginning in the Eocene (fifty-five million years ago), tectonic events lifted the ranges of eastern Panama, including the San Blas range. The axis of the range runs southeast to northeast and is dominated by the San Blas Fault, an escarpment notable for its length. Volcanic in origin, this broken landscape rises abruptly from 350 to more than 800 meters.

The geological characteristics of the coastal zone are similar to those of the mountains, with the exception of areas such as Punta Escocés, Punta Carreto, and Cabo Tiburón, where Tertiary formations (between twelve and sixty-five million years old) are found. The San Blas Archipelago is predominantly composed of coraline formations from the later Eocene.

Deposits of manganese (exploited during the First and Second World Wars), titanium, mineralized copper, gold, iron, and mercury underlie Kuna Yala.

Soils

The predominant soils in the region of Kuna Yala may be classified in very general terms as latosols, that is, clay soils characterized by their good physical properties: depth, porosity, drainage, and suitability for root development. Their chemical fertility, however, is intermediate to poor. Because of their low mineral content, they have little organic material and tend to be quite acid.

Even though the soils are poor, when the jungle has not been destroyed, they support an immense diversity of flora and fauna. A very efficient recycling process maintains the balance and the productivity of the natural forest. When forest cover is lost and soil management is inadequate, soil fertility deteriorates within a few years. This process is aggravated dramatically in similar areas outside of the Comarca, where there is extensive cattle ranching.

In Kuna Yala there are five distinct classes of soils. The best soils are found along the coast, particularly in the area of the Bay of Masargandí and at the mouth of the Gangandi and Mandi Rivers. An estimated 85 percent of the Comarca's soils are not arable and are more suitable for growing permanent crops and natural forests.

Topography

The topography of the Comarca of Kuna Yala is varied and irregular. Its most outstanding features include the San Blas range, the rolling hills from 100 to 200 meters in height that fall toward the coast, the plains near the shore, the islands, the Gulf of San Blas, and the continental shelf (fig. 4). The highest peaks in the San Blas range are Dianmaiyala (or Cerro Brewster), which, at 850 meters, is the highest point in the Comarca; Obu (747 meters); Ibedon (726 meters); Diablo (518 meters); Demardakeyala (668 meters); and Galedyala (765 meters). Outside of the Comarca, on the Colombian border, is Mount Tacarcuna (1,875 meters), important in the past because the Dule people took refuge at its summit from attack and natural disasters.

The Rivers

More than two-thirds of the planet's surface is covered by oceans. In fact, someone has said that we should call our world "planet water" rather than "planet earth." The land of the Comarca—and its culture—is strongly influenced by the rivers and the sea.

All of the rivers of the Comarca flow into the Caribbean Sea. There are more than twenty large rivers in Kuna Yala, the following being the most prominent: Armir, Carreto, Nabagandi, Achailadi, Guadi, Sangandi, Napsadi, Ogobgandiuar, Guanugandi, Ukupseni, Digandiki, Nargandi, Nuudiuar, Marsargandi, Gardi Seni, Gardi Dummad, Nergala, Gangandi, and Mandi. The rivers of the Comarca generally have beds fewer than twenty-five kilometers long and relatively small drainages, with certain exceptions in the western part of the Comarca (such as the Gangandi and the Mandi basins).

The rivers drop precipitously to the sea from the Continental Divide. As a consequence, there are hundreds of falls, cataracts, and rapids in their upper courses. In the rainy season, even small rivers may cause severe flooding. The waters are crystal clear except in a few areas where colonists have entered, as they have at the headwaters of the Gangandi

River. The mountain waters are relatively cold (23°C). In low-lying areas, rivers flow slowly. Here the average temperature of the water rises to 25 to 27°C. Unlike in the Pacific, in the Caribbean the influence of the tides is minimal, because of which there is little upstream penetration of salt water.

The Kuna obtain fresh water from the rivers. They make daily trips to the mainland to obtain fresh water for their homes. They also take advantage of the trip to do their laundry and bathe. Outboard motors must be turned off when canoes enter a river. Today there are aqueducts to a number of the major islands, so inhabitants of these islands no longer have to go to the mainland for fresh water.

Rivers are also used for travel between the coast and agricultural plots. They are fished by Kuna who live on the mainland and, especially when summer winds make ocean fishing difficult, by some island Kuna as well.

By means of the conservation of the natural forests and their watersheds, the rivers of Kuna Yala are among those with the best water quality in all of Central America.

The Sea

In and near the sea, the Kuna conduct a great part of their day-to-day activities. They obtain the majority of their animal protein and even the ingredients for their traditional medicines from the sea.

Along the coast of Kuna Yala there are a variety of marine environments: open sea, coral reefs, islands, mangroves, sandy and rocky beaches. The continental shelf is narrow (eight to seventeen kilometers). Islands vary in size and are less than a meter above sea level. Most of the islands are located within five kilometers of the coast, with the exception of the Kaimau islands (also called the Mauqui or Cayos Holandeses) located fifteen kilometers offshore.

The average annual temperature of the sea is 27.9°C , and varies from 24° to 31°C. The tide rises and falls an average of 33 centimeters. There are no coastal currents; beyond the continental shelf currents move west to east.

Marine biologists at the Smithsonian Institution estimate that the region contains one of the highest number of coral species in the Caribbean. Nearly sixty species of marine sponges are reported in the western zone of the Comarca.

An irregular coastline dominates the western extreme of Kuna Yala, between Punta San Blas and Cayos Cabeza—which includes the Gulf of San Blas and the Archipelago de las Mulatas. Numerous islands extend

Figure 4. Profile of Kuna Yala. (Ologuagdi)

outward into the ocean toward the border of the continental shelf. Between the islands of this area there are deep, wide channels that allow transatlantic cruise ships to enter. These channels also allow seawater to flow between the gulf and the open sea.

There is little geographical information about the next sector—from Cayos Cabeza to the Bahía de Carreto. Here, the continental shelf is narrower and falls over a short distance from roughly twenty meters to two hundred or more meters in depth. Between fourteen and seventeen kilometers from the coast one finds trenches from one thousand to twelve hundred meters deep. In the zone between Bahía Carreto and Cabo Tiburón the continental shelf is wide and shallow and extends toward eastern Colombia.

It appears that cultural adaptation to the marine environment has not had time to develop fully, since cultural activities endanger the sea's resource base in several ways. Species such as lobster (*dulup*), sea turtles—especially the hawksbill turtle (*yauk*)—certain shellfish, and even ocean fish have been under pressure from overexploitation. This pillage of marine resources is motivated by a constant and injudicious external demand and the Kuna's eagerness to make money.

The creation of adequate internal rules and real protection for certain marine resources has been discussed at length in General Congresses. Certain practices, such as the use of trawling nets and nets that do not discriminate on the basis of the size of the fish that are taken, ought to be controlled immediately to stop the depletion of populations of the marine organisms that sustain the Kuna. The Dule have the unavoidable responsibility of caring for the sea, stopping overexploitation, and moving quickly toward rational use. Their behavior will be judged by their children and grandchildren.

The Climate and the Seasons

Kuna Yala presents two types of climate: an extremely wet tropical climate in mountainous regions, and the humid tropical climate on the plains and parts of the coast.

Average temperatures vary between 26° and 27°C in low-lying areas to roughly 20°C at higher elevations. The average annual precipitation is between twenty-six millimeters to more than four thousand millimeters; it varies according to elevation. The relative humidity is high because of the trade winds from the north and east. Precipitation declines markedly during the summer months (January to April), and rain falls consistently in the winter (May to December).

The wind blows from different directions and at different velocities.

Table 1. Months of the Year

Month	Kuna Name	Meaning
January	Yolanii	Month of summer, of the Sun
February	Arinii	Month of the iguana
March	Dillanii	Month of the flowering of the Dilla tree
April	Ollornii	Month when the cicadas sing
May	Yauknii	Month of the hawksbill turtle
June	Masarnii	Month of the white cane
July	Bunurnii	Month of Bunur, a medicinal plant
August	Gignii	Month of the swallows
September	Apinii	Month of Apin, a medicinal plant

The Kuna name the winds by the directions from which they blow: *Sagir burua* ("coming from the Chagres River"), *yoor burua* (trade winds from the north, "winds of summer"), *dad nakue burua* (winds from the northeast, "from where the sun rises"), *yala burua* (winds from the south, "from the mountains"), *Mandi burua* (winds from the west, "from the Mandi River"), *dii burua* ("winds of rain," which blow suddenly before it rains and then stop just as suddenly), and *magad burua* (gentle winds from the northeast). (During the winter, when the *magad burua* blow, people comment: "Today it is not going to rain.").There are also local variations in the names for the winds, depending, in part, on the location of the community.

The names of the months of the year also refer to events that occur in nature (see table 1).

Vegetation

In comparison with the other nine provinces of Panama, the Comarca Kuna Yala has the greatest percentage of forested land. For the Dule children who have never left their territory, it would be difficult to imagine that the world is not green (fig. 5).

Before the construction of the road that goes from El Llano to Gardi, the vegetation of the region was one of the least known to western science because of its inaccessibility. The problem lessened as botanists used the El Llano–Cartí (Gardi) road. Before 1970, scientists collected specimens in Puerto Obaldía, Armila, Mandi, and on a very few islands. In 1983, however, botany students in PEMASKY's Project of Studies for the Management of Wilderness areas of Kuna Yala began to describe the flora in detail.[1]

The Comarca is of great interest to botanists because of its floristic relationship with the Chocó of Colombia, the Guyana highlands, and South America; that is, the vegetation of Kuna Yala is more related to that of South America than to that of western Central America. Some Panamanian plants are found only in the San Blas Range.

The Holdridge life zones present in the western part of Kuna Yala are classified in the following manner: starting at the sea and rising toward the mountains (the life zones change with altitude): humid tropical forest (only in the lowlands); very humid premontane forest (above the humid tropical forest zone, to 250 to 300 meters above sea level); very humid tropical forest (between 300 and 800 meters, the most common forest type in Kuna Yala), and premontane rain forest, found in the Comarca only at the peak of Cerro Dianmayala.

Deforestation and Ancestral Rights

Latin America and the Caribbean support high biological diversity in a variety of environments, including the largest expanse of tropical forest on the planet, almost eight hundred million hectares. More than two thirds of the species of flora and fauna on earth are found in the tropics, which means that the biological diversity of the planet is located in large part in a group of "developing" countries. It has been calculated that the American tropics support twice the forested area of Asia and three times that of Africa. Brazil alone contains 22 percent of the world's flowering plants. Colombia and Peru each support more than seventeen hundred species of birds; in the entire tropical region of the American continent there are forty-one hundred species of birds, or 45 percent of the world's avifauna.

The abundance of life in the region is a responsibility that should be protected and used rationally and not subject to the logic of a voracious market economy.

More than 90 percent of Kuna Yala is covered with forest. The region still has many pristine natural areas, but the destruction of tropical forests like these is a serious ecological problem, not only in Panama, but in all of the world's tropical regions.

Deforestation is also something of a problem in Kuna Yala. On the one hand, there are zones along the coast where the Kuna themselves have cut too much forest, for example, in wet areas where mangroves are cut to make drainage ditches for agricultural plots. On the other hand, there are sites where non-Kuna colonists have entered and developed extensive rangelands, for example, at the heads of Gangandi's rivers, near Nusagandi on the El Llano–Cartí road, and along the border with Colombia.

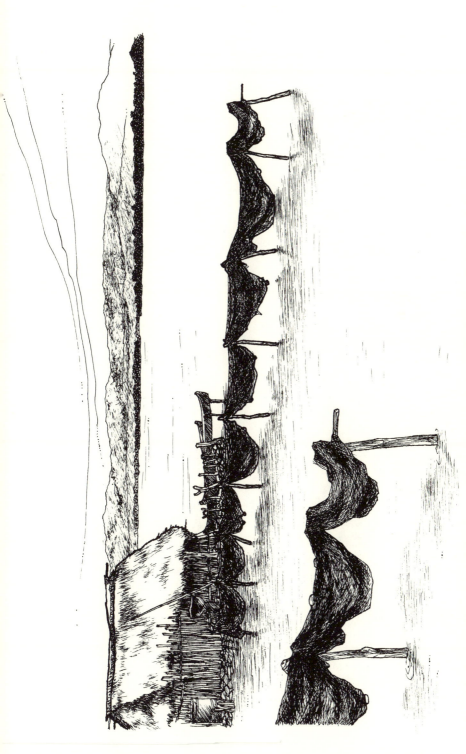

Figure 5. The Kuna Yala mainland as seen from the island of Gardi Sugdup. (Ologuagdi)

Indiscriminate deforestation threatens the territorial and cultural integrity of Kuna Yala. It is urgent that an immediate solution to this problem be found, via the legal mechanisms that defend the legitimacy of the Comarca. The situation is not nearly so serious as it is in the territories of indigenous peoples of the Amazon, however, because the Kuna own their land. No one who is not of Dule nationality may own land or resources in Kuna Yala.

To reaffirm these ancestral rights before the Panamanian state has not been easy. It has required a single-minded—and sometimes violent— struggle on the part of the native people and a particularly logical and

Figure 6. A Kuna man harvesting rice on his farm on the mainland. (Ologuagdi)

flexible stance on the part of Panama's political authorities. The Kuna keep these events in mind. Nearly all of the conflicts between Kuna and non-Kuna in the Comarca have been based on disputes over the possession of or profit from natural resources.

In 1915, the state established an Intendencia (regional office) on the island of El Porvenir. Since then, the Intendencia has assumed the role of administrative center in the Comarca. In the same year, schools, detachments of colonial police (as they were called), and dance clubs were established in Yanndup (Narganá), Dad Nakue Dupbir (San Ignacio de Tupile), and Ukupseni (Playón Chico).

In 1925 the Kuna rebelled against the abuses of the colonial police in what was known as the Dule Revolution. As a consequence, a treaty was signed with the Panamanian government and, five years later, the partial autonomy of San Blas was conceded. In 1938, Panama recognized the Kuna territorial reserve. In 1945, delegates from both the Panamanian government and the Dule people drafted the San Blas Charter (Carta Orgánica de San Blas). This legal document includes the naming of three chiefs (*caciques generales*) and formalizes the Kuna General Congress, a semiannual meeting of indigenous authorities from each of the communities. In principle, it is the General Congress that, through majority rule, sets the course of the Dule people.

The Charter also confirms the position of *intendente*, a public office that at the time was occupied by a non-Kuna appointed by the Panamanian government. Since the beginning of the 1980s, the General Congress has presented a slate of three of its own candidates from which the government chooses one to be *intendente*.

At the national level, the Panamanian Constitution of 1972 re-created the National Assembly of Representatives. San Blas was nominally divided into three districts (*corregimientos*), each with its own representative elected by popular vote. The Kuna also elect two delegates with the title of legislator to the National Assembly.

Since the beginning of the century, then, the Kuna have been modifying their governmental structure from a system of autonomous communities grouped into one—or more than one—fragile confederation (nominally linked to the nation-state of Panama) into a more complete and formal regional structure incorporated into a modern nation.

—Jorge Ventocilla

Note

1. Before the El Llano–Gardi road was built, botanists could collect only in more accessible areas. Some collections were made along the road during the 1970s and the early 1980s, but the first organized collection effort began in 1983.

5

Terrestrial Fauna

The Central American isthmus has always been the scene of migration and convergence of the fauna of Abya Yala. Therefore, part of the animal life that we find in the region is of South American origin—*bero* (sloth), *guigib* (anteater), *dede* (armadillo)—and part is of northern origin—*sugachu* (raccoon), *moli* (tapir), *goe* (brocket deer). In the jungles of Kuna Yala there are more species of birds, butterflies, and trees than are found in most European countries.

Throughout this book we will discuss the roles of various animals and their relation to the lives of the Kuna. In this chapter we describe seven forest animals from the mainland that are important to the Kuna, since it is these animals that provide most meat in the Kuna diet. We will also discuss how these animals are hunted by the Kuna.

Extensive and uncontrolled hunting (along with deforestation) is why many animal species in Panama are in serious danger of extinction. Hunting with dogs, in particular, has caused the disappearance of entire populations of game animals in many parts of the Panamanian interior. Hunting dogs are elements foreign to the forest and have been trained very successfully to pursue wild animals, which have not developed instinctive defenses against them.

In Kuna Yala dogs are almost never used for hunting. If the use of hunting dogs becomes more generalized in Kuna Yala—and there are indications that this is beginning to happen in communities close to the frontier of colonization—certain wild animals will not survive and the majority will become fearful and disappear from areas near human settlements.

The following descriptions are the result of both library research and the testimony of Kuna hunters and farmers, who have always lived in contact with the fauna of their land. We have shared hunting trips and long hours of conversation with them, and the experience has contributed to the reformulation and enrichment of our knowledge of the natural history of the Comarca.

Uedar

Uedar (collared peccary, *Tayassu tajacu*) is of particular importance to the Kuna because it is the wild animal that supplies communities with the most meat (fig. 7). Collared peccaries are a very social species and travel in groups of two to eight.

Their range and distribution covers a series of habitats. This very adaptable animal is found from Arizona in the United States to the Río de la Plata in Argentina. Its distribution in Panama includes forested sites and disturbed lowlands, and it is found in such areas throughout Kuna Yala.

In contrast to the northern race, which has been well studied, there is little information about the collared peccary of Central and South America. The animals that we have weighed in Kuna Yala average forty-seven pounds. In Costa Rica it is reported that litters are born in May, at the beginning of the rainy season. The *uedar* is diurnal, but may be active in the evening as well. In Gangandi, it is more often captured in fallow land or cultivated fields than in primary forest. The same is true in the Darién, where the indigenous Emberá and Wounaan hunt them on their farms, which are surrounded by forest.

The meat and the hide of the collared peccary are commonly used in many parts of their extensive distribution. In the Comarca the meat is used, but not the hide. In some communities the meat is a requirement for the celebration of the *inna*, the chicha festival.

Uedar is considered one of the pests that most disturbs Kuna crops, principally root crops such as yucca. Some farmers in the Gardi area believe there are now more *uedar* than before. They can be found all year in the cultivated areas, but in the summer, the land dries up and is harder to dig, so many of them move to higher ground.

It is said that the fruit of *igua* (*Dipteryx panamensis*), which ripens between December and January, is "special food" for the *uedar* because only it can break the tough outer seed coat.

We have even observed the hunting of collared peccaries in the sea. In June 1989, three peccaries were taken from the sea, two near the island of Pico Feo and one near San Ignacio de Dad Nakue Dupbir. Older Kuna say that such behavior is also observed among white-lipped peccaries and deer after an earthquake.

Yannu

The *yannu* (white-lipped peccary, *Tayassu pecari)* is similar in appearance to the *uedar* (fig. 8), but larger, sometimes reaching 110 pounds. The average weight of the *yannu* hunted in Gangandi was 66 pounds and the

**Figure 7. *Uedar* raised in captivity in the community of Gangandi.
(Ologuagdi)**

maximum weight reported for a female was 100 pounds. It has whitish
lips and lacks the characteristic collar of the *uedar*. White-lipped
peccaries live in large groups that may include more than one hundred
individuals. The groups roam constantly throughout the forest, covering
long distances between areas that they periodically revisit.

Figure 8. A herd of *yannu*. (Ologuagdi)

Yannu are omnivorous and are often seen feeding in areas where palms are abundant. They defend themselves aggressively and are considered dangerous. Their only natural enemies in Panama are the big forest cats such as the *achu barbad* (jaguar) and the *achu ginnid* (puma). It is said that the *yannu* is very sensitive to habitat disturbances in both highland and lowland humid forests and that, with the jaguar, they are the first large mammals to disappear when an access road is opened into a virgin area.

Little is known about their mating season. We have seen small *yannu* piglets in August and January. Some hunters claim to have seen males mount females as both run through the jungle without stopping. These hunters believe that the young are born when their preferred food, the *isberuala* (*Manilkara bidentata*) is in fruit. The *yannu* also likes to eat *igua* (*Dipteryx panamensis*) and *nalub* (*Bactris gasipaes*).

The *yannu* is one of the most symbolic animals for the Kuna. It is this animal that the older people speak of with the most reverence. A good Kuna hunter knows many details about the life of the *yannu*—where and what it eats, in which months it comes near their community, when it reproduces, and which individuals are dominant in the group.

It is said that the *yannu* has an odor of "burned earth" and that, although the *uedar* has a stronger odor, the *yannu* has a better sense of smell. Therefore, you have to "play with the wind" to hunt it. The older Kuna hunted *yannu* and *moli* (tapir) using pit traps. To check the traps, they did not get too close so as not to leave their smell and frighten the animals.

According to some Kuna hunters, there are two types of *yannu* bands, which can be distinguished by their tracks: the *no bravos* (nonaggressive) take flat steps and leave three-toed tracks; the *bravos* (aggressive) step more strongly and directly. In addition, the bristles on their bodies are raised. The differences between *bravos* and *no bravos* may refer to bands that have been frightened by a predator or by a party hunting the *bravos*).

If a hunter puts the scent of his breath or his armpits on a young white-lipped peccary, it will follow him as it would its mother. We have witnessed this in Gangandi.

Yannu spends more time in undisturbed forest and highlands and is not as attracted as *uedar* is to the Kuna's cultivated land. Nevertheless, we have seen quite a few *yannu* roughly three kilometers from the community of Gangandi, in an area of secondary growth. Seventy years ago, a banana company built houses near Gangandi, and today the *yannu* come to eat the flowers of the *uaa* palm (*Roystonia regia*) that were planted as ornamentals in front of the houses.

Kuna hunters consider the *yannu* to be an intelligent animal. According to them, three or four leaders run ahead and the others follow behind in several lines. In general, when a hunter sights a band, he returns to the community to recruit more hunters. If he sights the animals early in the evening, the group of hunters will go to look for them very early the following morning. After following the tracks the animals leave, the hunters make a decision about how to surround the animals; they are careful to note which way the wind is blowing.

The Kuna hunter who is in charge of the hunting party will rapidly position each hunter in succession (the first to be positioned will be the one who notified the rest of the presence of the *yannu*). When the person who is in charge finally "sits" with his back to the wind, he whistles like an animal they all have agreed on and the person who was positioned first takes the first shot. The animals come together when they hear the shot and at the third scream of their "leaders," they stampede. They may run for hours.

The *yannu* and the *ari* (iguana) are the only two animals that the Kuna hunt in groups. If the group does not get even one *yannu*, the men are embarrassed to return to the community empty-handed; since the *yannu* is a large animal, everyone in the community will be hoping to eat fresh meat when they return.

According to tradition, just as lightning over the sea marks the coming of the *yauk* (sea turtle), lightning over the mountains means that the bands of *yannu* are approaching. The *bakaka* (*Daptrius americanus*) also may announce their coming with its song. If someone dreams about soldiers, it is said that he will find a band of *yannu*. Once when we were accompanying a Kuna on a hunt, we told him that one of us had dreamed of a *yannu* the night before, and he immediately asked where we had sighted it in the dream.

According to the hunters of Gangandi, the populations of this wild pig on the Mandinga Plain dropped appreciably when the banana company came in the 1920s and cleared the forest. In addition, their own agricultural practices have eliminated the *yannu*'s food plants. A hunter from Gardi Sugdup commented on one occasion that on his island they do not make as many hunting forays as they used to because now the people prefer to shoot white-lipped peccaries as soon as they see them rather than return to announce their find to the other hunters; this may be because there are fewer hunters than there once were.

Some hunters are of the opinion that the *yannu* come closer to the coast during the dry season, when there is little water in the mountains. Two groups of *yannu* arrive in the Gangandi hunting grounds. One group comes along the coast, and the other group through the high mountains. The two groups originate from the two sides of the Mandungandi, on the Pacific slope. Because the Kuna are familiar with the routes that the white-lipped peccaries follow, the hunters from one community often advise those of neighboring communities to prepare because the *yannu* are coming in their direction.

In many areas of Panama, this species has been exterminated, whether directly through indiscriminate hunting, or through the destruction of its habitat. To maintain populations of *yannu* in Kuna Yala, no more animals than necessary should be killed. Furthermore, when the forests are protected, the home of the *yannu* is protected.

Usu and *Sule*

The *usu* (agouti, *Dasyprocta punctata*) is the forest animal that is seen most frequently in the lowland forests of Kuna Yala. The *sule* (paca,

Figure 9. *Sule* entering a streambed in Kuna Yala. (Ologuagdi)

Cuniculus paca), its nocturnal cousin, is larger—twice its weight—and can live at higher altitudes (fig. 9). The *sule* is also known as the *napanono* (earth head) in Kuna Yala. According to tradition, one must bathe after eating it, or feel lazy the following day. Both animals are quite timid and prefer to live in wooded areas near rivers and streams.

The *usu* plays an important role in the forest because it buries seeds when they are abundant, to feed on later. It does not always excavate all of the seeds in a time of scarcity; therefore, some seeds germinate and grow into trees. In regions in which indiscriminate hunting has eliminated the *usu*, certain trees cannot reproduce normally.

In the communities of Gangandi and Gardi Sugdup, four *usu* are required for the celebration of the *inna suid*. *Sule* are not required, but their meat is prized if it is available. Normally, Gangandi offers *sule* meat to visiting dignitaries.

The *sule* is nocturnal and lives in areas similar to those the *usu* frequents by day. Apparently, the *usu* feeds on agricultural crops more than the *sule* does. In Gangandi we have seen female *sule* giving birth at the end of September, the *usu* in February.

Both are sought after by hunters, and their natural behavior leads to their easy extermination when dogs are used, even without the use of firearms. This applies especially to the *usu*. In fact, Heraclio Herrera was able to grab an *usu* during a botanical expedition. If a dog finds one, the *usu* begins to run in circles without leaving its territory, thus facilitating its capture.

Goe

The *goe* (red brocket deer, *Mazama americana)* is not as well known in Panama as the *uasar*, or *goe bebe nikad* ("horned deer," white-tailed deer, *Odocoileus virginianus*). The *goe* usually inhabits dense forests, where it lives alone or in pairs (fig. 10). Its distribution in Panama includes all undisturbed forested areas.

The *goe* is reportedly common in the western part of Kuna Yala, although there are no good estimates of population in other parts of the Comarca. It has occasionally been seen eating crop plants. In Gangandi some people maintain that the meat of younger animals is not as tasty as that of the adults. One person from Gardi Sugdup told us that the *goe* is required for the celebration of the *inna suid* in this community, and that it can be replaced only by iguana.

Of all of the hunters whom we have interviewed, only two report having seen white-tailed deer in the Comarca. Apparently, this animal is uncommon in Kuna Yala. However, hunters recognize it if shown a photograph. Eustorgio Méndez, a zoologist, affirms that on the Carib-

Figure 10. A *goe*. (Ologuagdi)

bean slope of Panama the *goe* is found only at the edge of the region
bordering Costa Rica. Dan Janzen, a biologist who has worked for many
years in Costa Rica, indicates that there are a few uncertain observations
from low-lying areas on the Caribbean side of that country.

Some Panamanian campesinos say that the *goe* fights with the *uasar* and does not share the areas where it lives. It appears that the *uasar* finds disturbed or deforested areas more to its liking.

Moli

The largest forest animal in the Latin American tropics is the *moli* (tapir, *Tapirus bairdii*) (fig. 11). An adult may weigh more than five hundred pounds. The *moli* has a solid, muscular body and short, fairly thin legs. Its overall coloration is dark brown, paler on the belly and lower body. Its skin is quite thick, up to an inch thick on the back and rump. Short, coarse, but sparse hairs cover its body.

The *moli* lives in forested areas near rivers and swamps. Despite its appearance, it can run and jump when the need arises, and it swims with great dexterity. The *moli* is a solitary animal, although occasionally one may encounter the male and the female accompanying their offspring. The female gives birth once per year and usually has only one offspring, which stays with her until it is a year old. Between four and eight months of age, the young have a different coloration from the adults; that is, their skin is chestnut colored with white and tan spots and stripes. This coloration, similar to that of the paca and of fawns, provides camouflage when the *moli* are approached by a predator such as a jaguar. Their upper lip is extremely flexible and long, somewhat reminiscent of that of an elephant. Nevertheless, in evolutionary terms, the *moli* is related to the horse and the rhinoceros.

The *moli* is completely herbivorous, feeding on leaves, fruit, buds, and some seeds. It is primarily nocturnal, although it is possible to find it during the day. It travels through the same places, cutting easily recognizable paths.

The *moli* has poor vision but it is credited with a tremendous sense of smell and great auditory capacity. On the coast, it is often found in areas where mango trees (*Mangifera indica*) are in fruit. Farther from the coast, where mangoes are less common, for example, in Gangandi, hunters wait in *sua* trees (fig, *Spondias mombin*) for the *moli* to come looking for fruit.

The *moli* is one of the animals most sought after by hunters. In most of its range, it has been eliminated or is in serious danger of extinction, principally because it yields a great deal of meat. In addition, among the Kuna, the best hunters are recognized by the number of *moli* they have taken. Formerly, the meat of forest animals was divided among the members of the community (always among the children first), which contributed to the fame of a hunter in his community. Communities still exist in which the meat of the *moli* and other animals is shared; these Kuna villages are farther from the market economy.

It is not uncommon for active hunters to know who has shot the most *moli* in Kuna Yala. A hunter from Niadup (Digandiki) told us that he knows of only four hunters who have taken more than a dozen of these animals. To have shot more than three *moli* makes a hunter noteworthy in Kuna Yala.

Figure 11. *Moli*, **the largest terrestrial mammal in Kuna Yala. (Ologuagdi)**

Ari

Ari, the iguana (*Iguana iguana*), is a very important animal in the life of the Kuna. It is the only reptile that lives in trees (fig. 12); we see it on the ground only when it comes down to lay its eggs or to escape an enemy.

Figure 12. The *ari*, ever-present in the life and worldview of the Kuna. (Ologuagdi)

It eats the leaves, flowers, and fruit of forest trees. Its diet includes numerous plant species, but biologists do not know exactly how many. There are certainly trees whose leaves contain chemical substances that iguanas avoid.

As is the case with all reptiles, the internal temperature of the iguana is a function of the ambient temperature. Thus, we see the *ari* sunning itself in the treetops early in the morning and in the evening when the sun is setting.

Iguanas are up to 1.5 meters long, but, despite their relatively large size, they prefer to hide rather than to fight. If grabbed by a hunter, however, they will defend themselves by striking with their tail, biting, or scratching with their sharp nails. Basically, however, the *ari* is not aggressive and likes to live peacefully in the branches that sway in the breeze. The *ari* cannot live where there are no trees and prefers, in any case, to be in trees on riverbanks, so that if startled, it can hide in the vegetation or jump into the water.

Iguanas reproduce once a year. At roughly the end of October, they appear to be very restless and move about among tree branches. Males begin to establish and defend territories in the tops of trees, where they copulate with females. Younger males wait on the boundaries of the adult males' territories to see whether, by chance, they also can mate with the females.

Males defend their reproductive territories until the end of January. In February, females put their eggs in holes that they excavate in soft earth in areas without much vegetation; these are the famous *ponederos de iguana* (iguana hatcheries). In the interior, the *ari* is known by the nickname *gallina de palo* (branch hen).

Between April and June we find the recently hatched iguanas. It is common at this time of year for Kuna fathers who work on the *fincas* to bring back baby iguanas as gifts for their children.

The *ari* live not only in Kuna Yala but also in all other areas with appropriate environments, from Mexico to Brazil. In many places, natural populations of *ari* have diminished drastically because of uncontrolled hunting and deforestation. For our own good and the good of the iguanas we have to make sure that nothing like this happens in Kuna Yala.

The iguana is very important in the life of the Dule. It is present in their popular songs, in their legends, in the chants recited by the *gandur* in the *inna suid* ceremony, and, of course, in their diet.

—Jorge Ventocilla

6

Hunting in Gangandi

Most of Kuna territory has a broken topography, dissected by many short rivers that fall swiftly from the San Blas range to the coast (map 2). In general, there are no large, flat areas near the coast.

The area known as the Llanura de Mandinga (or Mandi) is an exception. This low-elevation plain covers over fifty square kilometers and is situated between the mountains like a flattened cradle almost nine kilometers long. Gangandi is located eight kilometers from the coast in the southeastern corner of the plain.

For at least a century, the coastal Kuna have migrated to do agricultural work in Gangandi. The first residents of *Gangandi* came from the islands of the Gardi sector—Narasgandup, Akuadup, Gardi Sugdup, and Urgandi—and from more distant sites, such as Yanndup and Usdup. Only at the beginning of the 1950s did Gangandi become a true Kuna community.

Two circumstances strongly influenced the environment and the pattern of human settlement on the plain: the establishment of a banana company at the beginning of the century, and, during the Second World War, the installation of a military base. We do not know how much cultivated land was ceded to the banana company. In aerial photographs taken in 1986, however, one clearly observes that on almost all of the plain, the forests are relatively young and are distinct from those of the foothills, where they appear to be older and less disturbed by human interference. The *saila* of Gangandi remembers his first impression on coming to the community as a child and seeing the banana company: "Everything had been transformed."

The people of Gangandi hunt in a place known as *uaa*, a name that they give to a West Indian palm (*Roystonia regia*) grown as an ornamental in the streets of Panama City and in the former canal zone. The *uaa* kept growing as the houses of the banana company fell into ruin and were overrun by the jungle. Now the hunters of Gangandi trap bands of white-lipped peccaries in this area.

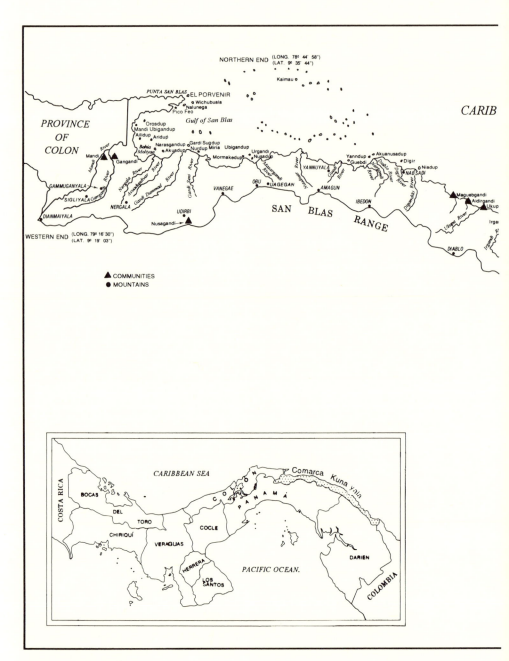

Map 2. Kuna Yala

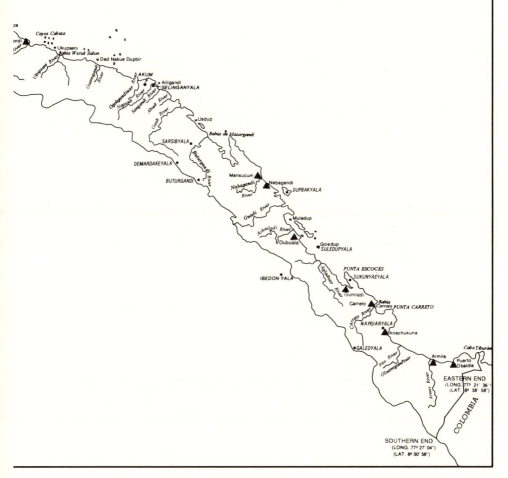

BEAN   SEA

N

Cayos Cabeza
Ukupseni
Bahia Weruk Sukun
Dad Nakue Dupbir
AKUM
Ailigandi
SELINGANYALA
Usdup
Bahia de Masargandi
SARSIBYALA
DEMARDAKEYALA
BUTURGANDI
Mansucum
Nabagandi River
Nabagandi
DUPBAKYALA
Guadi River
Muladup
Achailadi River
Dubuala
Goedup
SULEDUPYALA
PUNTA ESCOCES
SUKUNYAEYALA
IBEDON YALA
Gunnadi
Carreto
Bahia Carreto
PUNTA CARRETO
NAPGIARYALA
Anachukuna
GALEDYALA
Cabo Tiburón
Armila
Puerto Obaldia

EASTERN END
(LONG. 77° 21' 36")
(LAT. 8° 38' 58")

COLOMBIA

SOUTHERN END
(LONG. 77° 27' 04")
(LAT. 8° 30' 58")

The majority of the thirty-four dwellings that compose present-day Gangandi are clustered around the Congress and Chicha houses. The rest are scattered along both sides of the river for a kilometer along its western edge.

Most of the residents of Gangandi are related. Of the population of 279, almost half are children under twelve years of age. The surrounding land is used for agriculture, but the forest is not far from the houses.

In 1989, Rutilio Paredes, a forestry researcher from Usdup, and Jorge Ventocilla observed hunting practices in Gangandi for ninety-eight days. During this period, twenty-nine men from the community went hunting 156 times. Eighty-eight of these forays were successful.

Even though many men went hunting during our study, only five hunted regularly (with shotguns), supplying three quarters of the meat (fig. 13). In ninety-eight days, they killed 113 animals representing ten species: 71 iguanas, 13 collared peccaries, 11 pacas, 7 agoutis, 3 crested guans, 3 chachalacas, 2 coatis, 1 tapir, 1 white-lipped peccary, and 1 duck.

Most of the game was killed while the farmer-hunter was going to, returning from, or at his farm. All of the hunting in Gangandi takes place within a seven-kilometer radius of the community. The agricultural plots and the secondary forest (*nainu nuchukua*) were the sites most commonly used for hunting during our stay. For every ten successful forays, nine took place in one of these two areas, and six were exclusively on the *nainu*. These two observations are essential to an understanding of hunting in Gangandi.

Although hunting plays an important role in the nutrition and social organization of indigenous communities, there are very few studies of this subject in Panama. We have found that the Kuna in Gangandi are using resources in a sustainable way; thus, we can provide more information about what we will call "sustainable hunting" in the community of Gangandi.

The Kuna of Gangandi are not limited by either the quantity or the accessibility of game animals. Their hunting forays last only hours and may be accomplished in the course of agricultural work.

Of the species the Kuna consider edible, only the *sur ginnid* (red spider monkey), the *sur uega* (capuchin monkey), and the *yannu* (white-lipped peccary) are found far from the village. All of the rest can sooner or later be found within seven kilometers of the village. Even within ten minutes of Gangandi, tracks of tapir, collared peccary, paca, agouti, and brocket deer are found.

One might expect that the availability of game animals around Gangandi would be similar to that in any tropical forest area peopled by an indigenous group who practice slash-and-burn agriculture and who do

Figure 13. Kuna hunter on tree platform, with a headlamp for night hunting. (Ologuagdi)

not raise cattle. Nevertheless, the situation in Gangandi may be an exception. Peter Herlihy supplies us with relevant information from Lajas Blancas and other Emberá and Wounaan settlements in the Darién.

The indigenous people of Lajas Blancas do not carry firearms when they go to their farms, because larger game animals have been eliminated within a radius of a day's walk. Their hunting areas are far from agricultural and fishing areas, some are as far as twenty to thirty-five kilometers from the villages. To find animals such as tapir or white-lipped peccaries, the hunters of Lajas Blancas make trips to the headwaters of the Ucurganti River that last for a week or two, whenever their agricultural work permits. Herlihy has found a situation similar to that he observed in the Darién in regions inhabited by indigenous people in Honduras.

Hunting patterns in Gangandi indicate that inhabitants practice what Olga Linares terms "garden hunting."[1] By studying archeological remains, she reconstructed the life and subsistence practices of a small settlement of indigenous people in Cerro Brujo, Bocas del Toro, at about the time of Christopher Columbus's arrival. The site is similar to Gangandi: Caribbean, forested, and near the ocean. Linares observed that the animals most consumed in Cerro Brujo were species able to survive in areas modified by humans, and that, in some cases, they have higher populations under these conditions. By modifying their habitat, the ancient inhabitants of Cerro Brujo increased their provision of animal protein and hunted where they were harvesting agricultural products, thus the garden hunting concept. The same system is in use today among the Kuna of Gangandi.

Various ecological and cultural factors allow hunting in Gangandi to be a model for the utilization of natural resources that, for its environmental impact, we may consider a good model of sustainable use. The agriculture practiced in Gangandi (as described for the Kuna in general in chapter 3 of this volume) maintains a "mosaic" of vegetation of diverse ages and floristic composition. This mosaic attracts animal populations.

Every household in Gangandi has agricultural plots at several different sites, never all together. This production strategy may yield a variety of benefits. On the one hand, there is more security against natural disasters such as floods and hurricanes. In addition, the producer may plant different crops to suit the characteristics of different farms (soil, microclimate, location, and use). The vegetational mosaic may also help wildlife sustain their populations and eventually live closer to the farms, where they are hunted.

The fact that Gangandi is not more involved in the market economy prevents additional pressures on the land. In the case of the indigenous people of the Darién, Herlihy shows that, with their rapidly growing incorporation into the national economy via the Pan American Highway, they have been motivated to plant more land with marketable products (*ñame*—yams—in particular), and that they abandon the traditional cycle of agriculture and forest regeneration. Now, wide zones around populated areas are covered with grasses and weeds typical of zones with continuous burning and that are poor in game animals.

The abundance of primary forest near the community serves as a "nursery" for some animals hunted by the Kuna. The people of Gangandi are not putting more pressure on the forest, since most of the land actually dedicated to agriculture remains in the same flat areas that were cut seventy years ago by the banana company. There are few farms that are actually cut into the primary forest of the mountainous slopes. Approximately one fourth of the thirty-three farms established in the summer of 1989 were located in areas considered by the inhabitants of Gangandi to be primary forest.

In the secondary forests of the Mandinga plain live animals considered by certain authorities as inhabitants of isolated and little-disturbed forests, for example, the tapir, the white-lipped peccary, and the jaguar (fig. 14).

Experience in the Mandinga plain makes us aware that we still do not have a good understanding of the habitat preferences of certain tropical forest animals. Perhaps the forest and its animal populations recuperate more rapidly than is thought when there is neither cattle ranching nor overhunting.

The human population in the Gangandi area is minimal and, as such, there are fewer possibilities for overexploitation of the resource base.

The *galumar* (sites sacred in Kuna tradition) favor the reproduction and the sustainable harvest of game animals. In Gangandi some *suu* trees (*Ficus* sp.), which grow to enormous size along the riverbanks, are considered sacred—*galu*—and cannot be cut. The leaves and fruit serve as food for iguanas. Almost half of the iguanas killed during our study came from places with immense *suu* trees. This suggests that, by protecting the forest, the presence of animals is assured, which, at the same time, protects human food sources.

The sharing of meat promotes a perception of collective ownership of the forest wildlife. This attitude toward game animals favors their sustainable use. The practice of sharing meat is often found in hunting societies and is fundamental to their proper functioning. A hunter's decisions will depend on whether he hunts only for his own use or for other families as well.

In Gangandi the sale of wild game is not permitted, which is another way to avoid overexploitation. This is possible in large part because Gangandi is not immersed in the market economy. To the extent that money becomes more necessary for daily subsistence, as has happened on nearby islands, game becomes subject to the pressures of commercialization.

Hunting is probably no longer relevant to Kuna culture. It has become

Figure 14. Hunters returning to their island with a tapir captured the night before. (Ologuagdi)

a secondary activity in the Comarca. Today we sometimes observe that the coastal Kuna pay the Kuna from the Bayano region to supply meat for the *chicha* festival. The Kuna from the Bayano may bring game with them, or they may hunt in Kuna Yala under contract.

 Still, the Kuna certainly are eating more meat than are the campesinos who are colonizing the borders of Kuna Yala. "There is no game to be seen here," say the campesinos from San José and near the El Llano–Cartí Road, two areas where deforestation threatens the physical integrity of the Kuna Comarca. In the middle of extensive cattle pastureland, the campesinos no longer eat meat because of the destruction of the wildlife habitat.

Linares suggests that garden hunting may persist as a general practice in areas in which foreign influences, such as domesticated animals, arrived long ago. Our observations in Gangandi lead us to think that garden hunting will persist only where cattle pasture does not dominate the countryside and where both the forest and the traditions of the native peoples are maintained.

—Jorge Ventocilla with Rutilio Paredes

Note

1. Linares, "Garden Hunting in the American Tropics."

7

Money Creates Hunger

We the Kuna distinguish ourselves from nonindigenous peoples through our culture. Without money they cannot move, they cannot eat, they cannot drink, they cannot sleep. For this reason, they are destroying the natural world with respect to the future of their children. They take no notice of the damage that they are doing. I maintain, therefore, that money makes people poor, that it creates hunger.

We the Kuna work the earth, alternating the planting of crops with allowing the land to rest for three or four years. Thus, we say that Mother Earth is changing her clothes when people cultivate different crops or trees. One thing that the indigenous peoples do not do is to leave the earth without protection and let it dry out. For this we must take care of our territory. We must prevent the colonists from invading.

Nele Kantule said: "The sea, the reefs, the fish are ours, and no one may take them from us. We must fish only as necessary. We have all of the freedom to use what nature gives us, but without taking more than is essential."

Our wise grandmothers took great care of all that surrounded them, above all the home, the family, and all that was shared: crabs, fish . . . If anyone in the family had a good catch, he shared. No one sold anything, and they gave just to give. But now, it's all money. I have to buy fish and crabs. The same is happening with deer meat, peccary meat. The hunters do not share meat the way they used to; instead, they sell it.

These days, lobsters are caught indiscriminately. Once our mothers placed an entire lobster on our plates early in the day. Likewise, the fathers ate lobster in the evening when they came home from work. Now, if you want to eat lobster, you have to buy it, if you have some money . . .

And the divers, when they sell lobster, they use the money to get drunk. These young guys are destroying the lobster population for nothing!

The young people think that they can make a living only from the sea.

The *sailagan* ought to counsel the young people, to tell them that they ought to fish in a way that will not finish off the lobster populations in Kuna Yala and that they also ought to go plant crops on the mainland.

We the Kuna do not destroy the forest. And when it is cut, we plant it again, stems of mango, avocado, guavas, and trees such as caoba for timber. The road that leads to the Nele Kantule Elementary School is going to be planted with mangoes and avocados because they attract the water and also, we will have trees that will feed our people.

I regret that the Comarca is losing its personality. Baba is not going to take it from us; we will lose it ourselves. We are following the *uaga* and it seems to me that no one will stop the change.

We give our votes to our legislators so that they will defend us and speak up for us. But now I do not even know them. It would seem that we are resigned to what is happening to us. Everything's peaceful. No one says anything. If we were more aware, we would notice the loss of our values—principally of the earth, because without her we cannot survive—and we would not be so peaceful.

Baba entrusted us with the earth because we would live on her like a big family. But we are becoming less unified, now we do not see ourselves as a family. True, when the electoral campaigns begin, then they remember us. Even so, during the local and general congresses I have noticed the absence of representatives of two, even four, communities.

I realize that the authorities keep the women out of political positions: it seems that we are fit only for the kitchen. Only the men meet to address the problems of the Comarca. I wonder: Why don't I speak Spanish? I wish that I had studied until sixth grade so that I could say what I feel. I could better defend my Comarca.

—Elvira Torres, community leader in Usdup
(Recorded by Valerio Núñez)

8

Submarine "Deforestation"

Hunting in Kuna Yala also extends to marine animals, particularly lobsters, aquarium fish, and turtles. Overexploitation of marine fauna in Panama has reached alarming levels. As Olaidi shows later, the overfishing of marine faunal resources occurs because of ignorance, complacency, and shared culpability of players both inside and outside of the Comarca.

This overexploitation is definitely motivated by the greed of the *uaga*, that is, by unscrupulous interests outside of the Comarca. It is equally undeniable that it is up to the Kuna to protect the base of their existence. This process begins with a detailed knowledge of the country's marine fauna.

The Lobster

The traditional name given to the lobster is *olouidoegingya*, a name that is still commonly used. Lobsters live in groups in the *akua biski* (coral reefs), caves, and marine rocks. They hide by day and emerge only at night to search for food. Lobsters eat principally sardines and clams, but also worms, crabs, shrimp, sea urchins, sponges, and fish. They are becoming rare in some places and in others they have completely disappeared.

The Kuna know very little about this animal. Information about the lobster should be disseminated to save the animals, not only for their own sake, but also because they are an important food resource. In particular, a standard should be set that requires the immediate release of a lobster with *mutu sichid* (black spots), because it will soon give birth.

The waters of the Comarca of Kuna Yala provide a habitat for five types of lobster: *dulup* , the common lobster (*Panulirus argus*); *angi*, the spotted lobster (*Panulirus guttatus*); *dulup arad*, the green lobster (*Panulirus laevicuada*); and two flat-bodied lobsters generally known as *uisi* (*Scyllarides aequinoctialis* and *Parribacus* sp.).

The Genus

Lobsters are invertebrates. Male lobsters have a padded opening in the base of each palp. Female lobsters have two additional claws or hooks at the end of each palp and an additional pair of swimming palpi under their tails.

Mating Season

Most lobsters mate and lay eggs when the ocean is warm. In the Caribbean (and in Kuna Yala) most animals mate and lay eggs between March and July. The male and the female lobster face each other when they mate. The male puts a sticky liquid on the female's abdomen. This sticky liquid hardens and forms a black spot, which contains a great quantity of sperm.

Egg Laying

The female lays many brilliant orange eggs, which she guards under her tail. While laying the eggs through small apertures between the third pair of palpi, she rubs the black spot and thus frees the sperm, which then fertilize the eggs. The female sticks the eggs to very fine hairs on the swimming feet under her tail. A lobster carrying her eggs this way is sometimes called "berried" or "strawberried" because her eggs look like thousands of tiny berries.

The female carries the eggs until her offspring hatch. She protects them from being devoured by fish and, at the same time, fans them with water. The eggs die if they are removed from her tail.

After one to four weeks, the small lobsters are ready to leave their shells. Now the eggs are a dark maroon color.

The female lays more eggs than will grow and mature. A female with a back (the area extending from the horns to the beginning of the tail) thirteen centimeters long may lay approximately three times more eggs than an animal with a back nine centimeters long.

"Floating Lobsters"

Recently hatched lobsters do not look at all like adults. Their flat, transparent bodies have large, thin palpi. They do not walk on the bottom; rather, they float in ocean currents for six to twelve months.

Most marine creatures float in the ocean at birth. Thus, in the first stages of their lives, lobsters drift about in the company of juvenile conchs, crabs, clams, and small fish. This marine population is collectively termed "plankton." Most plankton is too small to see with the naked eye; nevertheless, it provides an important source of food for larger marine animals.

After six to twelve months as plankton, the lobster undergoes another change—called metamorphosis. A juvenile lobster can swim actively and it moves closer to the coast. Young lobsters become established in shallow areas such as mangrove swamps, in sea grasses, or on shallow coral reefs. They also hide in the algae that grows on the bottom of boats, on anchor lines, and on dock supports. Soon after they become stationary, their transparent body becomes pigmented. Now, their bodies are covered with pale yellow and brown spots.

One almost never sees young lobsters when they are floating in the ocean. The first point at which they are visible is when they become fixed in one place and acquire their coloration, which explains the belief that young lobsters have just emerged from their eggs. In fact, by the time one sees it, the lobster is roughly a year old.

The lobster is defenseless at birth. Because only a few survive, a female lobster must lay thousands of eggs. Most are eaten by other animals. Red snapper, sharks, and manta rays eat larger lobsters. They are also the favorite food of squid, grouper, and nurse sharks. Nevertheless, as lobster is one of the favorite dishes of humans, we consume more lobster than any other animal.

Habitat

Lobsters live in shallow areas among algae and sea grasses. Mangroves and sea grasses are essential as feeding areas. As small lobsters grow, they move toward the coral reefs, where they reproduce.

Only juvenile lobsters are found in certain places. The popular explanation is expressed in such comments as "in this place the lobsters grow only to a certain size." This is an erroneous impression, because lobsters move to other areas when they grow larger.

Age and Size

Water temperature influences the growth rates of lobsters and the time it takes them to mature. Most lobsters begin to mate when they are between three and five years old. At this age a lobster measures approximately 20.5 to 25.5 centimeters in length from head to tail. The back measures at least 9 centimeters in length. By measuring the length of a lobster's back, one can determine if it has reached reproductive age.

A lobster continues to grow throughout its life. It may live for more than forty years and reach almost a meter in length from the head to the

tail. In areas where lobsters are fished as soon as they mature—after three
to five years—one never sees animals so large or so old.

The Molt

The hard shell of a lobster does not grow as the lobster grows; rather, the
animal occasionally abandons its old shell and makes a new one—the
process of "molting." Before the molt, the lobster forms a tender shell,
like a second skin, beneath its hard outer shell. When the lobster molts,
the old shell opens at the point where the tail meets the rest of the body,
and the lobster moves backwards and exits through this opening.

At this point, the lobster has only its soft, skinlike shell, which
stretches and slowly hardens. The lobster now has space to grow inside
its new, hard shell, until the time comes to molt again.

The Endangered Marine Fauna of the Comarca of San Blas

by Olaidi

The commercial exploitation of lobsters in Kuna Yala has given rise to
many polemics. One hears of "overexploitation" and illegalities on the
part of businesses from within and outside the Comarca, as well as a lack
of consensus and an "inability to regulate" on the part of the traditional
Kuna administration. Kuna individuals and organizations interested in
the protection of the environment have made meritorious—but only
partially successful— efforts to halt this abuse of the Comarca's natural
resources.

Kuna who are now more than thirty years old remember that in their
childhood it was normal to eat lobster three or more times a week and
if you wanted to eat lobster, it was only a matter of going out to find one
nearby. Now there are no more lobster in the Kuna diet.

Everything changed at the end of the 1970s and the beginning of the
1980s, when small planes from Panama City began to arrive to buy
lobster in the Comarca. At first, buyers, fearing the reaction of the Kuna,
were cautious and came infrequently (once every week or two). Large-
scale commercialization began in 1984. In 1994, there were daily flights,
even on Sundays.

The Kuna *langosteros* (lobstermen) remember that years ago they
could capture twenty to thirty, sometimes up to forty, lobsters in a day
by diving on a single reef at depths of three to five arm lengths. Today,
they take four to eight lobsters per day, and then only by searching
several reefs and diving much more deeply than they did before.

Underwater Crime

In slightly more than ten years, the lobster has been converted into Kuna Yala's principal export . The Kuna are killing their lobsters to satisfy consumers outside of the Comarca and the country while the Kuna diver is left with relatively little to show for his efforts. Outsiders know little or nothing about the significance of overfishing in the territory of an indigenous people who survive on the products of the sea.

There are no studies of the commercialization of the lobster and its effects in Kuna Yala or in the rest of Panama. Complacent Kuna authorities and, it appears, an uninterested central government in the capital contribute to the problem. We tend to forget what we cannot see. The destruction of the tropical rain forest is something that we can see with our own eyes; thus, it provokes protest. Submarine "deforestation," however, may advance without provoking the least reaction, simply because we cannot see it.

The sea as habitat is as fragile as a tropical forest. Experts tell us that there are two fronts in the struggle for the survival of our species: one is the tropical rain forest, the other is the sea.

The Lobster's Road to Gethsemane

Small planes land at all hours on sand and gravel airstrips in Kuna Yala (fig. 15). They are not coming to pick up passengers bound for Panama City; they pick up lobsters and, more recently, seafood of all types, which will end up in the elegant restaurants on Contadora Island, in Panama City, in Miami and Madrid.

Planes land at Paitilla Airport in the capital city, often at dusk, after the few government inspectors have finished their shifts. The "contractors" of these flights are not required to present detailed information regarding their cargo. The Kuna themselves have no idea how many lobsters they have sold. The Directorate of Marine Resources of the Ministry of Business and Industry has some information regarding the number of lobsters sold and additional details of their commercialization, but its information is inexact.

Lobster fishing takes place from mid-March until mid-December (fig. 16). During the summer months, climatic conditions make it very difficult for divers to work on the open ocean. In general, three or four Kuna, almost always young, daring men, fish from a dugout canoe with an outboard motor. One stays in the dugout while the rest dive for lobster. Unlike in other parts of the Caribbean, the Kuna search for lobster during the day, not at night.

Figure 15. Every day, small planes fly between Panama City and Kuna Yala to pick up lobster shipments.

Lobster fishing requires a great deal of physical endurance, because it begins early in the morning and lasts until early afternoon. The diver's equipment consists of mask, snorkel, fins and a long rod made of *ila* with a wire slip knot at the end. Kuna lobstermen are not organized into cooperatives or "grupos de producción" (production groups), as the Kuna often are in agricultural enterprises.

The most expensive lobster—and the most sought out by the divers—is the common (or spiny) lobster. For every ten lobsters taken, four to six are this species. The green lobster, which is roughly the same size and looks very much like the common lobster, is caught occasionally. The spotted lobster is the most common in the Comarca, but it is much less prized because it does not have high market value.

Lobsters are sold by the weight of the whole animal. The pilots who come to pick up the lobsters become merchants as they engage in commercial transactions on the airstrips of each community. They pay in cash: $3.50 per pound for spiny lobster or green lobster, $1.25 per pound for spotted lobster. The prices vary according to the quality and size of the animals and supply and demand.

Negotiations involve Kuna intermediaries, almost all of whom have another business, such as a store, a bakery, or a small food concern. Intermediaries prefer cash in dealings with the small planes, but some-

Figure 16. Female lobsters laden with eggs are trapped indiscriminately.

times they receive perishables such as chicken and meat, sausages or cheese, or cases of beverages in exchange for lobsters.

The relationship between the intermediary and the lobstermen is defined according to whether the latter have the necessary equipment for lobstering (fig. 17). The lobsterman works independently if he uses his own equipment (dugout, outboard motor, and fuel), or he may depend on

Figure 17. The diver's modest equipment contrasts with the business-man's resources.

the intermediary to lend him equipment. The intermediary pays the independent lobsterman $3.40 per pound for spiny lobster or green lobster and $1.00 to $1.10 for spotted lobster. If the diver uses the intermediary's equipment, he receives only $3.00 to $3.25 per pound for spiny lobster. Kuna who do not have the means to feed their families often make an arrangement with an intermediary to exchange food for some of the lobster.

Some divers prefer to deal directly with the pilots. These divers usually lack motors for their dugouts and cross the sea by paddling (*canaleteando*).

Lobsters awaiting sale are kept in wire cages or in larger "corrals" (*dulup galu*) built in the water (fig. 18). While transactions are under way on the airstrip, the lobsters are kept in nylon sacks.

The lobsters' journey from the Caribbean to the Pacific begins when, thirty minutes to an hour later, they arrive at Paitilla Airport. The pilot sells the merchandise to another intermediary, who sells it to restaurants, hotels, and packing plants for $8.00 per pound. Processing plants, in turn, may export lobster for $18.00 to $20.00 per pound. Some planes fly directly from Kuna Yala to Contadora Island in the Pacific, where lobsters are sold to stores and hotels for up to $12.00 per pound.

Figure 18. Lobsters may be held in cages for several days before they are shipped.

At each step in the process of commercialization, the humble lobster increases in value. It leaves the plate of the Kuna to be transformed into an exotic delicacy inaccessible to mere Kuna.

The Hunter and His Prey

Lobstering in Kuna Yala is a difficult and dangerous job. The only weapons the lobsterman has to fight the dangers of the sea are physical stamina and a harpoon. Their risky occupation (as distinct from that of the rest of the Kuna, who do agricultural work) and their access to almost immediate cash (and their use of it) have made the divers almost a caste in Kuna society. A diver averages $175 per month, an appreciable sum in local terms, but far from enough to satisfy his basic needs and those of his family.

To work on the open ocean means, divers tell us, headaches, ear infections, and, sometimes, skin infections, symptoms that are easily tied to excessive exposure to sunlight and contact with salt water. One thousand Miskito lobstermen in Honduras have been paralyzed recently as a result of inappropriate use of diving equipment.

In the Comarca, sharks have injured or killed lobstermen. For example, in 1989 in Kaimau, a lobsterman was attacked by a shark and lost his left arm. In Dad Nakue Dupbir a diver was attacked by a shark and died as a result. Years ago, a shark attacked another diver, who was miraculously saved despite being gravely wounded. And at the beginning of 1993, another diver died on the open sea, this time not devoured by a shark but by the sea itself.

Divers are not looked on kindly, nor are they understood for what they are: a link to a business in which others, including other Kuna, take the biggest piece of the pie. All divers know that their lobster is eventually sold—for fabulous sums—to hotels and restaurants as far away as Europe. But everyone is ignorant of how much the intermediary makes on the lobsterman's labor. One witness, a lobsterman, told us : "The guy in the airplane promised me an outboard motor if I got more lobsters, and food from the city, and even new diving equipment worth $80, if I would keep quiet and not ask for a raise in the price of the lobster I sell."

The ability of Kuna lobstermen is famous outside of the Comarca. Kuna divers work on Contadora Island. The species they take in the Pacific are similar to those they catch in the Caribbean, but much smaller. The Pacific contractor offers the diver all of his equipment and $8.00 per pound. Some Kuna divers work independently in Contadora and sell their product directly to hotels and restaurants for up to $12.00 per pound. Other Kuna work in Santa Isabel (Colón Province), in Bocas del Toro, and in Veracruz, near Panama City.

Ironically, although the quality of lobster in Kuna Yala is the best in the country, it is comparatively poorly priced. It is easier to get a better price near the market where it is consumed, although the quality of the lobster there is inferior.

In Kuna Yala lobster is caught and sold regardless of its size, sex, or reproductive state. The only market "prohibition" is imposed by the purchaser, who will not buy lobsters that are too small to resell. And we all turn a blind eye to this plunder and destruction of a marine resource.

Rational Commerce

The Kuna must understand the lobster problem as part of a broader problem that includes economic, cultural, and social aspects. Kuna society is beginning to commercialize its marine resources at a dizzying rate for purely mercantile and exploitative reasons.

Overexploitation for internal consumption has practically finished off schools of *mila* (tarpon, *Megalops atlanticus*). The products of the sea, including lobster, other seafood, and aquarium fish, have become valuable only as merchandise.

Instead of selling nothing, the Kuna must learn to sell rationally. In other countries in the Caribbean, the regulation of lobster fishing—including the enforcement of quotas during the reproductive period—has permitted the orderly and sustainable commercial use of the crustacean. To do this, it is essential to study the life cycle of the lobster.

Of roughly thirty divers whom we questioned, only three could determine the sex of a lobster; the rest could only guess, using the presence of eggs or size (they mistakenly thought that the male was bigger than the female). Others in the group do not know the significance of the black patch, and some even think that it indicates that the lobster is male.

Divers are aware of the decline of the lobster and are willing to cooperate if there are new regulations; however, they have families and are committed to an occupation that pays immediately, in cash. Thus, we must achieve an equilibrium between the use and the protection of these marine resources. The best way to push for fair pricing and to gain control of the quantity of lobsters that are taken is by organizing, perhaps into lobstermen's cooperatives or production groups. Perhaps the Kuna General Congress could serve as the intermediary between lobstermen and the non-Kuna buyers. Central gathering (and control) points could be established under the Congress's supervision and administration. Only lobsters of legal size and only females that are not carrying eggs could be sold. A closed season could be established to include the months from March until July, when most mating and egg production take place.

A Direct Flight to the Aquarium

Kuna divers, using lures and harpoons for underwater fishing, also catch fish, spider crabs, squid, conch, and sea turtles. When they want to capture squid, they dump chlorine bleach into the animal's hiding places to force it to leave its cave. Invariably, the bleach also causes the death of small squid.

A marine biologist believes that the inappropriate and extensive use of chemical substances (fish tranquilizers) and other kinds of commercial chemical substances, be they Clorox, agricultural insecticides, or petroleum and its derivatives, contaminates marine flora and fauna. As a consequence, the life and reproductive cycles of ocean inhabitants are affected, which, in the end, result in the death of many animals. In some cases, commercial chemical substances used in excess accumulate in animal tissue, primarily in the liver and in fatty tissue. Later, when these animals are eaten, the human organism is affected.

For some time, divers have devoted themselves to getting shark fins and live ornamental fish, which are sold to an intermediary who exports them to North America.

The sale of marine organisms for aquaria began in November 1992. Witnesses affirm that such commercialization is now so common that the major concern is not the wanton exploitation of the animals, but the price they fetch. Even children are beginning to work in this business.

Collectors of marine fauna are primarily looking for exotically colored and shaped fish, anemones, soft corals, and particularly beautiful clams. The same divers and lobstermen and their intermediaries are involved in this activity, which is so lucrative for the intermediaries and dealers in Miami. One source told us in July 1993 that in his community "the small fish are being sold like crazy."

No one in Kuna Yala knows the magnitude of this business, neither how many animals are dying when they are captured, nor how many survive the trip to the aquarium. They are transported from the Comarca to Panama in polyethylene bags and foam boxes into which oxygen is bubbled. All of the equipment for transport is provided by the international buyer and the Kuna intermediary, once he has taken a short course in management and shipping tropical fish. One witness told us: "The ornamental fish buyer travels weekly to the communities, giving three hundred dollars to the Kuna intermediary to purchase tropical fish." The Kuna General Congress intervened in May 1993 to stop the trade and never to sell these resources to outsiders.

Turtles Unlimited

The Kuna government has also been unable to stop the overexploitation of marine turtles. The Kuna call May *Yauknii*, that is, the "month of the hawksbill turtle." In May, the turtles come to the beaches of Kuna Yala to lay their eggs. The Kuna have always harvested turtle eggs. Rules prohibit taking more than half of each laying, and in the past, the Kuna did not even kill the turtles. The Kuna used to believe that turtles were human beings punished by Bab Dummad and that whoever killed a turtle ran the risk of contracting tuberculosis, because the spirit of the animal would invade the *burba*. There are still older Kuna who, for these reasons, do not eat turtle.

But times change, and today, the Kuna eat both turtle eggs and meat. As in the case of lobsters and ornamental fish, the extent to which turtles are exploited is set not by the subsistence needs of the indigenous people but by the demand of the external market. But hoping for self-control on the part of outside commercial enterprises with the idea of establishing sustainable harvests is utopian. It would seem that there are no limits to the thievery of commercialization without a conscience.

In June and July of 1993, the marine turtles returned. In one community in far western Kuna Yala, however, a group of divers realized that the *morro* turtles, which are not eaten in this area, could be sold to people on boats who would take them to the eastern part of the Comarca, where they *are* eaten. The divers captured *morro* turtles in huge numbers, using *ila* rods with a wire slip knot and underwater nets.

Although their sale is prohibited by national law, these turtles are sold for ten dollars or more for an entire live animal, or for fifty cents per pound of meat. The product moves to places as distant as Usdup via Kuna boats, Colombian trading boats, and official government launches (fig. 19).

What Is to Be Done?

It would seem that when a plant or animal can be converted into money, human beings forget their cultural principles. Not everyone is willing to stand up for the principles that the elders in the Congress House sing about in the evenings. But, who is going to speak for the turtles if not the Kuna themselves? Are the lobster, the fish, and the turtle in the sea to satisfy our needs or our ambitions?

If there is one thing that characterizes Kuna society, it is the Kuna's ability to adapt and to maintain themselves. The situation with lobsters, seafood, reef fish, and turtles will require adaptation. Certain Kuna organizations are very clear about this issue. At the level of the General Congress and the Traditional Congress the will to make a decision and to follow through exists. Conservation groups in Panama will support Kuna initiatives to protect and manage marine resources. As a people, the Kuna have overcome difficult situations in the past. They have always been strong when they act together to defend the earth. Now the Kuna must unite to defend the sea and its inhabitants.

—Jorge Ventocilla with Olaidi

Figure 19. Turtles are taken with machetes, lines, and government boats, without regard for traditional taboos.

9

The Spirit of the *Uaga*

All things come from Mother Earth. Nothing exists that is more necessary than she is. Without her, life is not possible. Our ancestors fought for her because they recognized her value. "I am nothing without the earth. I would be poor without her," so they said.

We do not destroy nature. We do not have the tools to do that. It is our tradition not to drastically alter the natural world. Our ancestors made their own tools—both for their homes and for their work. In this sense we certainly were not backward. The arrival of Christopher Columbus arrested our development. We stagnated. But we did not lose everything.

In the beginning the Europeans were not a highly advanced society. Little by little they broadened their knowledge—until now. They advanced while we, lacking the means to exploit our resources, stagnated—until now.

I don't know how many ships there are in the world. But when their smoke rises to the sky it damages the atmosphere and the clouds change color. Our ancestors told us long ago to take care of the air.

Our ancestors didn't suffer from so many diseases. They developed a lot of taboos to keep their society under control. The foreigners don't have taboos like ours. Therefore, their behavior is strange from our point of view. The various diseases that come to us torment the world. Measles, smallpox, and polio, as well as AIDS and cholera, are all diseases that were formerly unknown in Abya Yala. They are the evils that their progress has brought us.

We always left medicinal plants in the fields when we cleared and cut trees. The elders give us advice about how to take care of useful plants. Therefore, in Kuna Yala we still have forests. The foreigners don't do this. They thoughtlessly destroy nature for their livestock.

The jungle and the forests provide us with meat, as well as vines, poles, and medicinal plants. In them lie our history and our culture. We know that Europeans don't have the same resources because their scientists come to the Comarca to see what is in our forests. I want it to stay this way, but I'm afraid that one of them will arrive with a chainsaw.

The lobster traders are responsible for the deterioration of our marine resouces—only for the money. Even if we want to control the fishing of lobsters, we won't succeed, because the young people who are involved in this activity are making their living from it.

Our tradition of working together no longer exists. Once, when a decision was made to address a problem, everyone complied unanimously. Now they follow money. We are acquiring the spirit of the *uaga*.

Once everything is evaluated in terms of money, it changes one's way of being, it makes one selfish. So said our forefathers. Thus we are beginning to deceive our forefathers. That's what I think.

—Cacique General Carlos López
(Recorded by Valerio Núñez)

10

Medicinal Plants

Between 1987 and 1990 I conducted an ethnobotanical investigation in four communities in the Comarca of Kuna Yala. The accelerated disappearance of traditional Kuna knowledge of herbal medicine provided the incentive for compiling and returning this cultural legacy to its original owners: the Kuna people.

The account of traditional Kuna medicine that follows is purely descriptive and should not be used as a manual for medical treatment.

Plants have always played an exceptional role in the lives of indigenous peoples. The science of native peoples reached an advanced level before there was a destabilizing force in their relationship with nature. In traditional medicine, people knew which plants were useful as cures for disease. There was, to one extent or another, an intimate relationship between people and their environment and a respect for nature that guaranteed the survival of many indigenous peoples.

In Abya Yala this historical evolution reached an impasse as a result of the European invasion. The native peoples were forced to retreat into more inhospitable and infertile areas. At the same time, native cultures began to decline. The way of life and the belief systems were irrevocably altered.

Now scientists and environmental organizations are sounding the alarm because traditional knowledge and the cultures of indigenous peoples are disappearing even more rapidly than their tropical habitats.

The prevailing atmosphere in a Kuna community in the Comarca of San Blas at the beginning of this century was described in 1990—shortly before his death—by Felipe Arias, Kuna botanist from the community of Ukupseni:

> All that we could hear in the streets of town were the melodic songs of the great *nelegan* and botanists in training sessions with

their disciples. Every afternoon after our work in the fields was done, each went to the house of his master to practice what he was teaching. There were always groups of ten or fifteen young people learning some medical specialty, or some healing treatment or chant. We stayed for several hours in training sessions. In any Kuna community it was routine to hear the specialists chanting in different parts of town. The house of our botanist and *nelegan* was our church, our school, our gathering place.

According to the Kuna way of thinking, medicinal plants were sent by Bab Dummad, who advised his spirits to defend the life and the soul of the Kuna. As a result, all of the plants in the forest are medicinal. Plants originated from the union of Great Father and Mother Nature (i.e., the earth, called Napguana in Kuna). Napguana, or Nana, gave birth to the first plants, the trees. These trees were invested with special powers. Great Father decided to send the plants first, before sending people, to prepare the environment.

Kuna botanists were exceptional people. They were dedicated to their science and had unshakable faith in the cures and in their ability to overcome evil spirits. The presence of the *nelegan* and botanists in Kuna communities is of great importance because they personify the struggle to resist the evil spirits that give rise to diseases and epidemics. The absence of these people represents the annihilation of the Kuna people and the death of their culture.

The *inadulegan* were in great demand among the people, which motivated the *inadulegan* to learn more and improve their specialty. Consequently, they practiced medicine rigorously and painstakingly. They sought out and collected medicines in the most remote areas of virgin forest, where they found plants that people had not disturbed and that, therefore, had stronger and much more effective medicinal properties than medicinal plants from disturbed areas.

Kuna medicine is broad and diverse: medicine practiced using plants (herbal medicine—see table 2) is distinguished from healing performed with chants. Treatment that involves the use of animal parts, inert objects such as minerals, and pieces of glass is also practiced. Herbal medicine and chants are administered daily, even when the treatment involves animals or inanimate objects. One complements the other. Treatments may be practiced separately or simultaneously.

In herbal medicine the substances that are prescribed, called *ina*, are plants and their different parts. The specialist who prescribes and administers herbal remedies is the *inaduled*.

Kuna treatments often involve the use of "medicinal baths." The *inaduled* prepares an infusion of bark, roots, leaves, or flowers in fresh

Table 2. Ailments and Remedies

Kuna Name	Description
Bina nunmaked ina	Medicine for liver pains
Burwa (sugued)	An ailment characterized by dizziness and vertigo. In severe cases the patient presents symptoms of epilepsy, such as convulsions, spasms or even fainting spells
Gammu ina	Medicine to treat inflammation, pains, or sore throat
Gammu ya	Sore throat
Garnunmaked	Pain symptomatic of arthritis or rheumatism
Gurgin ina	Literally "hat medicine." Medicine for treating problems related to the head (i.e., that require psychotherapy). Used to treat headaches, nightmares, fears, worries or neuroses, and also to stimulate intelligence
Ibya ina	Medicine for the eyes (ophthalmological treatments)
Igar obured	Literally "turning off of the road." Medicine for the treatment of bad dreams or nightmares. Also administered during pregnancy to prevent complications during labor. Plants used in *gurgin ina* may also be used in *igar obured*.
Ina gobaled	Plants used in preparation of beverages
Ina obaled	Baths prepared with medicinal plants
Ina waled	Plants used as incense or in steam baths
Musirgan nunmaked	Kidney pain
Naibe ina, dub ina	"Snake medicine." *Dub* (or *duba*, literally "cord") is the word used as a name for snakes. Refers to plants used to treat snakebite, used in baths, or used in psychotherapy to avoid thinking about snakes
Nig kannoed	Literally "soul invigorator." Refers to plants used as stimulants, to make women fertile, or to treat impotence
Oaged	Plants used to induce vomiting or as purgatives
Odammiboed	Plants used to treat fever
Oina	Medicine to treat colds and influenza
Sadib ina	Medicine for diarrhea
Siamar ina	"Women's medicine," that is, plants used to treat women's pain and during pregnancy

Table 2, cont.

Silisilit	Refers to asthma. Characterized by constant cough and shortness of breath. Called "dog sickness"
Sor noed	To defecate with hemorrhaging; hemorrhoids
Uka ina	"Skin medicine"

water either in a bucket or in a small dugout canoe. Using a cup or gourd, the patient pours water over the body. These ritual dousings are performed several times daily for twenty to thirty days for minor ailments, and for up to six months if the problem is more serious. Every four or five days, the *inaduled* changes the water or adds fresh herbs.

The *nele* is in charge of the diagnosis of diseases and determining their cause. The *nele* also crossed over to practice herbal medicine like the *inaduled*. The *inaduled* may specialize in certain fields of medicine such as treatment of fractured bones, snake bites, ophthalmology, wound healing, or sterility and fertility problems. Generally, within medicine as a whole, different levels of specialization are recognized. One of these, *ina burui* ("little medicine"), treats minor ailments such as stomachaches, headaches, colds, and skin inflammations. *Ibya ina*, ophthamological treatment, *muu ina* (also known as *bundor ina*), specialization in pregnancy or labor, and *nia ina*, treatment of people who suffer from epilepsy, are recognized specialties.

Formerly, a Kuna herbalist mastered several specialties while living with his teacher and accompanying him as he collected plants. Thus, the disciple was trained in collecting methods, how to distinguish the important plant parts, and the prayers of favor or speeches to the spirit of the plants. In the house of the *inaduled* the disciple was trained in the preparation of medicines, their proper doses, and the corresponding sicknesses or pains to be treated.

The student paid for his apprenticeship by hunting or by gathering plantains or wood, by fishing, or by providing fabric, molas, necklaces, and other articles. Patients also paid for medical attention in kind. Now payment is made in cash.

Today, traditional medicine has been drastically altered. As one Kuna botanist notes: "There are few botanical specialists who remain in the Comarca." They are the living libraries, and, if we do not take pains to save them, their knowledge will be lost forever.

The threat to traditional knowledge is worsened with the introduction of western education into the Comarca. The young see their elders as old-fashioned and superstitious.

Botanical Terms

The following table of botanical terms (table 3) will make it easier to understand the subsequent descriptions of thirty plants we have chosen of the three hundred medicinal plant species that we identified in Kuna Yala. The plants were all collected from the coastal lowlands of the Comarca near the communities of Gangandi, Gardi, Miria Ubigandup, and Ukupseni. We have chosen to represent a variety of life-forms (herbs, vines, epiphytes, and medicinal trees). In each description, we include the Kuna name as used by the *inadulegan*, followed by the life-form's scientific name and the plant family to which it belongs.

Table 3. Botanical Terms

Name	*Description*
Alkaloids	Nitrogenous substances of plant origin, basic in character, and often toxic, e.g., caffeine, nicotine, atropine
Arecaceae	Botanical designation for the palm family
Aril	Fleshy seed coat
Bract	A modified leaf that subtends a flower or inflorescence
Capsule	Dry fruit that splits open at maturity to release its seed
Chordate	Leaf or other plant part in the shape of a heart
Corm	Subterranean stem similar to a bulb
Endemic	Native to a certain geographic area
Epiphyte	Plant that grows on another plant without taking nutrients from it; generally has no roots in the soil
Follicle	Dry fruit that splits open only along a ventral line
Frond	The leaf of a fern
Genus	Group of plants or animals species that, in systematic theory, is the level of organization between species and family
Hemiepiphyte	Plant that grows partially on another and that has roots that reach the soil
Inflorescence	Flowers of a plant
Infructescence	The fruit that replaces the flowers on an inflorescence
Latex	Exudate produced by some plants; generally a milky color

Table 3, cont.

Leaf blade	Expanded part of a leaf
Leaflet	The parts of a compound leaf
Liana	Woody, climbing vine that often does not support itself and may grow up into the canopy on other trees
Petal	Part of floral whorl or corrolla, often brightly colored
Petiole	The stalk of a leaf that connects it to the stem
Pinnae	Part of a pinnate leaf (i.e., a leaf composed of several leaflets arranged along a common axis)
Plumule	Embryonic shoot emerging from an embryo, in this case, from the seed
Raceme	A simple inflorescence of pedicelled flowers on a common axis
Resin	Chemical compounds formed by terpines, esters, alcohols, phenols, and resinic acids; generally yellow or chestnut brown in color; insoluble in water
Rachis	Central supporting part of an inflorescence or of leaflets in a compound leaf
Rosette	A group of leaves arising from a short stem forming a radiating cluster
Spadix	Inflorescence with small flowers clustered on a fleshy central axis
Stamen	Male reproductive structure of a flower

Esnargan (*Acrostichum aureum*) (Pteridaceae)

This terrestrial herb with a short, stout stem has leaves that originate at the base of the stem and may reach three meters in length. Leaves are divided into pinnae, roughly thirty centimeters long and five centimeters wide. The lower surface of the pinnae of young leaves is covered with round, brown structures known as "sori," which contain the spores by which this plant reproduces.

Esnargan naturally occurs in coastal zones, frequently along riverbanks of Kuna Yala among the mangroves and in sites flooded by salt water. Its range includes all of tropical America.

The leaves of *esnargan* are used in medicinal baths as treatment for dizziness, vertigo, and headaches. A paste of tender fronds is placed in the nostrils of infants to treat colds and to clean out mucus that blocks breathing.

Figure 20 shows, at left, the life-form of an entire plant. Notice the pinnate, expanded leaves and the new, rolled fronds. At right is a detail of the venation of a sterile pinna.

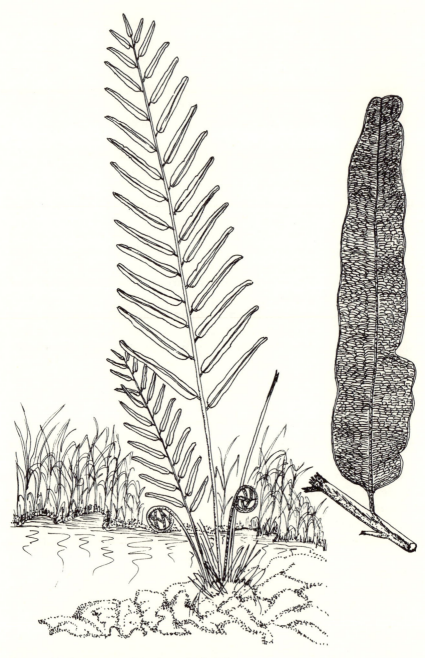

Figure 20. *Esnargan*. (Enrique Tejada)

Dior nugargid (*Cyathea petiolata* [Hook.] Tryon) (Cyatheaceae)

This plant belongs to a group of tree ferns with erect stems up to several meters (feet) tall. The specimen we collected in the forest of Gangandi had a stem twenty centimeters tall, with fronds three meters long. The genus *Cyathea* grows in mountain and hillside forests and is found in wet lowland areas of Central America and southern Mexico, in the Greater Antilles, and in Argentina.

The stem and the root are cut in short pieces and are used in medicinal baths as a remedy for aches and pains such as those caused by rheumatism and arthritis.

Naibe ugia (*Tectaria vivipara* Walker and Jermy) (Dryopteridaceae)

This is a terrestrial fern without a visible stem. Its frond consists of simple, entire leaflets. Its basal leaflet has an enlarged lobe. This fern, which is found only occasionally in the forest interior, usually grows on stream banks and in rocky areas. *Tectaria* is the most common genus of ferns found in the humid forest.

It is used as a psychotherapeutic agent to prevent people from thinking about snakes. The fresh leaves are used to prepare medicinal baths or are left to dry at room temperature for later use in steam baths.

Nidirbi sakangid (*Anthurium ochranthum* K.Koch) (Araceae)

This plant is a terrestrial herb up to 1.3 meters tall. The leaf, which is triangular and deeply lobed at the base, looks like a ray fish. The flowers are located on an elongated structure called the spadix and are bright yellow when mature.

Nidirbi sakangid is found in forests from sea level to two or three thousand meters in altitude, from Costa Rica to Panama. In Kuna Yala it has been reported in Gangandi, the El Llano–Cartí Road, Ukupseni, and Ailigandi.

It is used in medicinal baths in the treatment of psychological problems (*igar obured*).

Figure 21 shows the plant habit. Note lobed leaves and flowers blooming on a short stem, which is held above the soil line by its roots.

Nidirbi sakangid (*Anthurium subsignatum* Schott) (Araceae)

This epiphytic plant grows on tree trunks and branches. The leaves, which are lobed at the base, have a peculiar shape, a morphology

Figure 21. *Nidirbi sakangid.* **(Enrique Tejada)**

comparable to that of a sting ray when it moves with its fins extended.
Thus the Kuna name for this plant means, literally, "sting ray fin." The
inflorescence is elongated and green when immature, yellow at maturity.

It is found in the lowland forests of the humid tropics from Costa Rica to Panama. In Kuna Yala it has been collected in Gangandi. The roots and the leaves are used in medicinal baths in cases of snakebite and to treat dizziness. The popular belief that *nidirbi* cures dizziness and vertigo may come from the plant's ability to grow on trees and to tolerate heights and survive storms.

Abior (*Dieffenbachia pittieri* Engl & Krause) (Araceae)

This herb, between forty and fifty centimeters high has leaf petioles with dark green spots. All plant parts produce a very strong, irritating odor when cut.

Abior has been found only in Panama. It is common along the banks of the Gangandi River, in other disturbed or open areas, and in shady sites in the lowlands. It has also been collected at two thousand meters above sea level.

The sap contains abundant oxalic acid, which gives the plant its characteristic odor and burns the skin. The stem and macerated leaves are cooked and the extract is applied as a lotion to treat peeling skin. It is also recognized as an effective remedy for other skin irritations. The leaves, dried at room temperature, are powdered over a flame and used as talc to be rubbed onto the affected parts. In addition, medicinal baths of *abior* combined with pieces of spiny palm (*Bactris* sp.) are used to treat general aches and pains.

Some people hang this plant in the entrance of their homes to scare away bats. It is also said that the plant can drive away evil spirits.

Some Kuna farmers claim to have effectively used the plant to control leaf cutter ants and other ants that attack yucca and banana crops. They place pieces of *abior* inside the entrances of leaf cutter nests. Others cook the leaves and stems and then pour the extract into the ant nests.

Figure 22 shows the habit of the plant. Notice the leaf scars on the stem and the inflorescences among the leaves.

Naibe Uar (*Dracontium dressleri* Croat) (Araceae)

This herbaceous species grows to 1.5 meters in height. The leaf petiole has brown rings and spots and resembles a snakeskin. The fruit extends out over the ground.

Naibe is found only occasionally in the forest. Its geographical distribution extends from Costa Rica to Panama. In Kuna Yala it has been collected in the vicinity of Gangandi, in Nusagandi, on the El Llano–Cartí Road, and in Miria Ubigandup. In Gangandi and Miria Ubigandup it was cultivated near the residences of the herbalists.

Figure 22. *Abior*. (Enrique Tejada)

The corm is grated and mixed with water. The resulting beverage is used to treat throat irritations. A warm extract obtained by cooking the petiole and leaves is used to wash out wounds caused by snakebites. This plant is extensively cultivated in Kuna gardens.

Mammar dubaled (*Philodendron brevispathum* Schott) (Araceae)

This hemiepiphytic plant with scaly brown bark and chordate leaves is rare and was collected only a few times in the Canal Area of Panama and in the province of Colón. In Kuna Yala it was collected in the vicinity of Ukupseni in flooded areas.

Baths using the stem are employed to invigorate weak and sexually impotent men. In ancient times, a cooked extract of the stem was used to poison "crazy people" (epileptics).

Figure 23 shows, left, a stem segment, a leaf, and a young inflorescence (spadix), and right, its characteristic leaf shape.

Gugdar (*Xanthosoma robustum* Schott) (Araceae)

Gugdar has a well-developed trunk up to two meters tall. Its leaves are long and broad. When cut, they exude a whitish sap. *Gugdar* is common on rocky terrain along the banks of the Gangandi River.

The leaves are cooked and the extract is used as a lotion to treat irritated skin. A powder made by crushing and burning dried leaves is used for the same purpose.

Figure 24 shows the plant habit: a thick trunk and fruits developing among the leaves.

Gurgur sapi (*Himatanthus articulatus* [Vahl]. Woodson) (Apocynaceae)

Gurgur sapi is a tree twenty meters in height. The fruit is elongated and has two follicles. It was collected near Ukupseni and is also found in South America. The trunk and the leaves produce white latex.

To treat sores and skin ulcers, the Kuna apply the latex directly to affected areas. They also employ baths prepared with the bark.

Figure 25 shows, at left, a branch of this tree with leaves and fruit; at right is the plant habit.

Guabeu (*Malouetia isthmica* Mgf.) (Apocynaceae)

This tree, seven meters in height, is found in forested areas near Mandi, Gardi, and Ukupseni. It has white flowers and its bark exudes a milky sap.

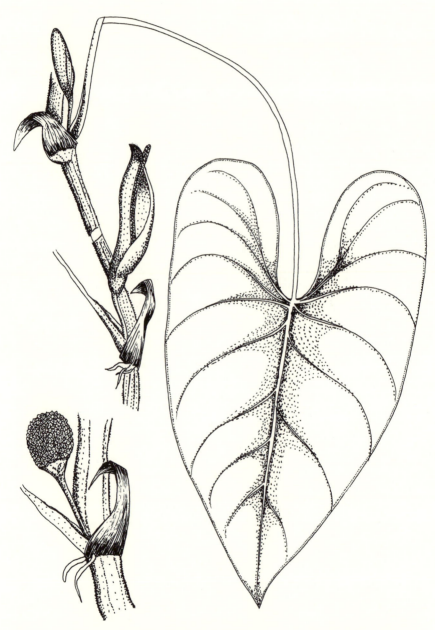

Figure 23. *Mammar dubaled.* (Heraclio Herrera and Enrique Tejada)

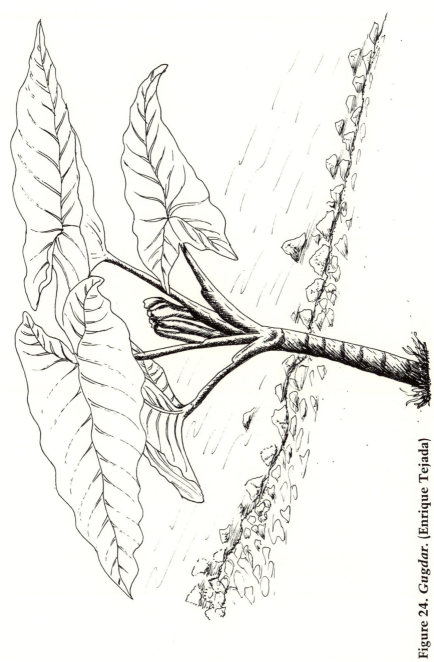

Figure 24. *Gugdar.* (Enrique Tejada)

Figure 25. *Gurgur sapi.* (Heraclio Herrera)

Pieces of bark are steeped in fresh water for no longer than a day. The resulting solution is given to people who have been bitten by snakes. The bark is also used to prepare medicinal baths for children suffering from diarrhea. The milky sap of the bark is applied both internally and externally to the throat to relieve inflammation and soreness.

Dingugia, ina gaibid (*Neurolaena lobata* [L.] R. Br.) (Asteraceae)

This herb grows to two meters in height in open areas, usually in agricultural fields. It is found from southern Mexico to Panama, Colombia, and Ecuador. The surface of its leaves is asperous and their margins are serrate. Larger leaves are characteristically lobed. Its highly branched inflorescence bears yellow flowers. Kuna botanists take advantage of its very bitter flavor for curative practices.

This is one of the primary plants used in the treatment of snakebite. The stem and leaves of the plant are boiled and the extract is used to wash the wound for the next five to seven days.

The cooked extract is also used as a lotion to treat skin inflammation and other general body irritations.

Figure 26 shows a portion of a branch with leaves and flowers. The biggest leaves, at the base of the plant, are characteristically lobed.

Dubsangid (*Aristolochia pfeiferi* K. Barringer) (Aristolochiaceae)

This climbing vine has chordate leaves and is covered with very fine hairs. It has recently been collected in the mainland forests near the community of Ukupseni and was previously collected only on Santa Rita Ridge in the Province of Colón.

The cooked extract from the stem and leaves is used to wash skin sores and wounds caused by snakebite.

Figure 27 shows a stem segment with a pubescent leaf and the fruit. The latter is characteristically split into six parts to allow the wind-borne seeds to escape.

Musguar, Yala guarguadid (*Protium* sp.) (Burseraceae)

This treelet is roughly ten meters in height. Specimens were collected on the mainland of Ukupseni. Several species of *Protium* are native to Panama. Its trunk, when cut, exudes copious turpentine-scented resin.

The resin is collected from the bark and made into a ball for storage. Shavings are mixed with water and taken as a remedy for colds, the flu, and asthma. The bark is also used as a purifier when bathing infants and as a cure for skin irritations.

Figure 26. *Dingugia.* (Ologuagdi)

Ueruer sorbi dubgid (*Gurania makoyana* [Lem.] Cogn.) (Cucurbitaceae)

This vine in the squash family has lobed leaves and yellow flowers held in very noticeable orange bracts. It is found in the lowlands in the forest interior.

The cooked extract of the entire plant is used for washing snakebites.

Figure 28, upper portion, shows a stem segment with leaves, an inflorescence, and a tendril. This structure allows the plant to climb. The lower part of the figure shows the viney habit of an entire plant.

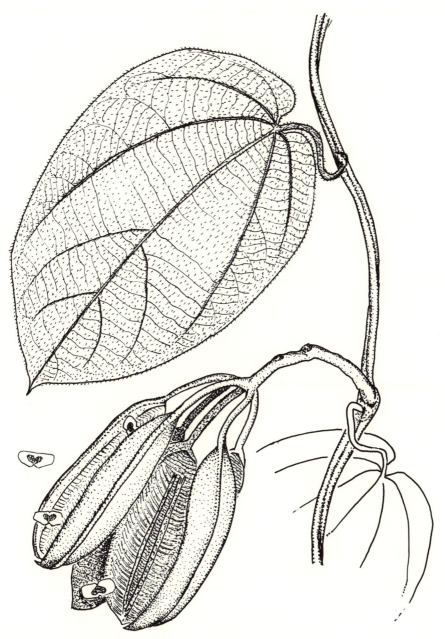

Figure 27. *Dubsangid.* (Enrique Tejada)

Figure 28. *Ueruer sorbi dubgid.* (Enrique Tejada)

Beno (Pachira aquatica Aubl.) (Bombacaceae)

This tree reaches up to fifteen meters in height. The flowers are large with elongated white or yellowish petals and numerous stamens. Its brown fruits are also large, up to thirty centimeters long. Its compound leaves have from five to nine leaflets arranged in the form of an open hand. Often found in the lowlands, it is common along rivers throughout the Kuna Comarca. Its range includes tropical forests from southern Mexico through Costa Rica and Panama to Peru and Brazil.

Botanists make a bark extract that is later used as a lotion to treat skin inflammation and abscesses.

Figure 29, above, shows the plant habit and a fruit; below, buds and an open flower with numerous stamens.

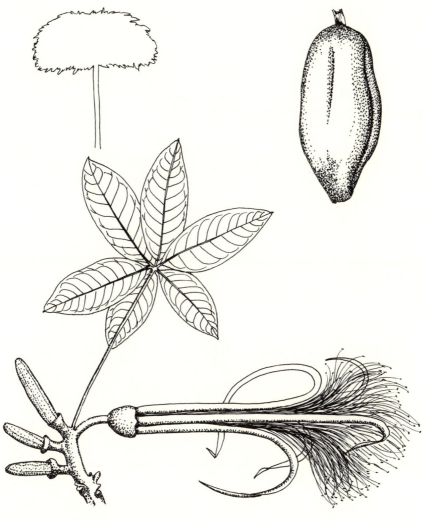

Figure 29. *Beno.* (Enrique Tejada)

Guiba (*Jatropha curcas* L.) (Euphorbiaceae)

This lobed-leaved tree, four meters in height, produces watery latex. It was collected in Gangandi as a cultivated plant from the garden at the home of the *inaduled*.

The green fruit is grated and mixed with water. The resulting beverage is taken to induce vomiting. The use of this plant may cause liver damage.

Figure 30 shows a branch with leaves and globose fruit.

Oluka dubaled (*Clidemia epiphytica* [Triana] Cogn.) (Melastomataceae)

This vine climbs tree trunks. It has small red flowers and is frequently found in all areas of the Kuna Comarca at various altitudes. The Kuna of Gangandi call this plant and other species in the same family *oluka*.

Bunches of this plant are used in medicinal baths for children as a remedy for drooling and frequent sweats.

Figure 30. *Guiba.* (Enrique Tejada)

Surmas (*Compsoneura sprucei* [A. Dc.] Warb.) (Myristicaceae)

This small tree has a thin trunk three meters high and a greenish inflorescence that develops into a capsular fruit that opens by splitting down the middle to reveal a single seed with a red seed coat. It is found in forests at various altitudes.

The stem is used to make dolls, which are later grated and added to water. The drink is administered orally to pregnant women before labor. The bark, leaves, and stem of young plants are used in medicinal baths in the treatment of epilepsy. In popular Kuna belief, epilepsy results from possession by animal spirits.

Bachar (*Pothomorphe peltata* [L.] Mig.) (Piperaceae)

The piper family includes many species: *Piper culebranum, P. glabrescens, and Pothomorphe peltata*. All are well known in Kuna Yala. They are herbs of varying heights up to three meters and are found in lowlands and mid-elevation forests.

The most common use of these plants among the Kuna is as a treatment for snakebite. When a patient comes in, the *inaduled* immediately sends someone out to look for a branch of one of these plants, which he will boil in water. A warm extract is used to wash the wound. Treatment takes four to seven days and during this period, the doctor/herbalist collects plants every day to make fresh extract. *P. culebranum* is also used in medicinal baths as a remedy for body aches.

Pothomorphe peltata (L.) Mig. is an herb fifty centimeters tall. Its leaves are round and lobed with veins extending from a center near the base. Figure 31 shows an adult plant with leaves and inflorescences.

Guandulu (*Pentagonia wendlandii* Hook) (Rubiaceae)

This shrub has a thin stem up to 2.5 meters tall. Its large leaves may grow to be 1.2 meters long and 50 centimeters wide. It is found occasionally in the forests of Kuna Yala. This plant is well known in Panama and Costa Rica.

The *inadulegan* use the bark of the stem and the leaves to treat snakebite. They boil plant parts and use the extract as a wash for the wound. This treatment takes five consecutive days, and the *inadulegan* must find fresh material daily. To strengthen the treatment, the bark and the leaves are also used in medicinal baths.

Figure 32 shows an adult plant approximately four meters tall. At the lower left is a fruit with persistent (attached) calyx. At the lower right a leaf shows the characteristically ear-shaped (auriculate) leaf base.

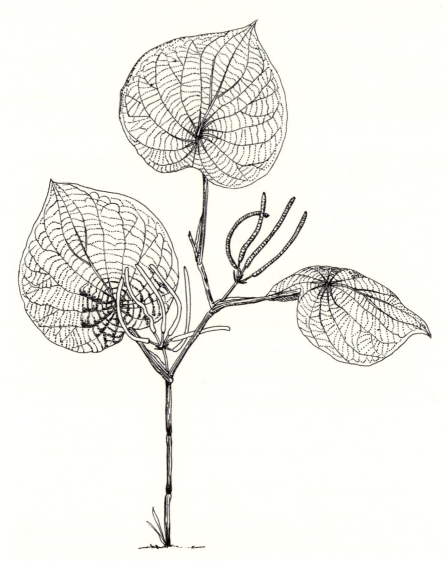

Figure 31. *Bachar.* (Enrique Tejada)

Iko nasi, Gannir iko (Randia aculeata L.) (Rubiaceae)

These bushes are 1.5 meters tall, with white flowers and small green fruit. They are common on islands and on mainland shorelines in the Kuna Comarca. Pieces of the plant are used in medicinal baths to treat body aches and pains. The branches are used as hooks for cups and household utensils in the kitchen.

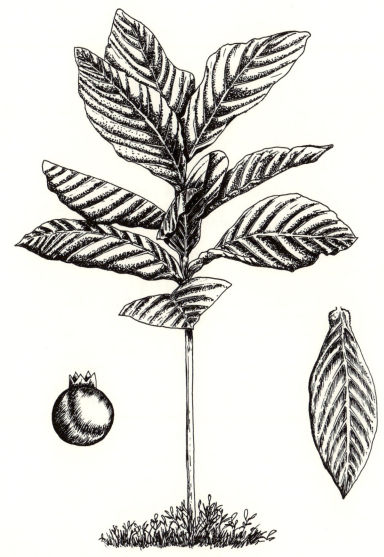

Figure 32. *Guandulu.* (Enrique Tejada)

Morgauk, Inaguag (*Sapindus saponaria* L.) (Sapindaceae)

This tree is fifteen meters tall and has brown fruit with sticky pulp. It grows in forests and on riverbanks in the lowlands of Kuna Yala. Its range extends from Mexico to South America.

In the past, the Kuna used the bark to alleviate colds and flu, although this practice is rapidly disappearing.

The bark and the fruit produce soap. The Kuna ancestors used it for laundering their clothes.The fruit is reportedly used as barbasco for fishing in rivers.

Ina gaibid (*Simaba cedron* Planch.) (Simarubaceae)

This thin-trunked tree four meters in height has brown fruit that contains a white seed. Its horizontally arranged rosette of pinnate leaves makes it stand out in the forest. It is found from Gangandi to Ukupseni. It is native to the Americas, where its range extends from Costa Rica to Colombia.

If one were to list the medicinal plants preferred by the *inadulegan* and the Kuna people in general, *ina gaibid* would be close to the top. The extract of cooked seeds is administered in small sips in the morning for four consecutive days for the treatment of snakebite. The grated seeds are also administered to treat gastrointestinal pain. An extract of the bark is used as a lotion to treat body aches.

On a research expedition between 1845 and 1881, botanist Dr. Berthold Seemann noted that this was probably the most well known tree among the natives of New Granada because its seeds were prized as an antidote for snakebite and the bites of scorpions, centipedes, and other poisonous animals. According to Seemann, the natives of the region wore the seeds on a chain around their necks or carried them in their tobacco pouches. Similar information has been reported by researchers who have worked among the Kuna in the Darién and in Kuna Yala.

Udud bungid (*Quassia amara* L.) (Simarubaceae)

This bush is 1.5 meters in height and has red flowers. The leaves are pinnate with a winged petiole and rachis. This bush has characteristically bitter bark. In Kuna Yala it grows in the forests of Punta Porvenir. It is also found from Mexico to Panama and in northern South America.

This plant was brought from Punta Porvenir and cultivated in Gangandi by *nele* Roberto Pérez. The experience of *nele* Pérez demonstrates the validity of the cultivation of certain traditional medicinal plants.

The stem and leaves of the plant are cooked and the extract is administered in small sips from morning until evening for seven days to treat snakebite. In other parts of America the bark is used as a remedy for diabetes.

Figure 33 shows a branch with two leaves, each of which has five leaflets. At left is a raceme of flowers.

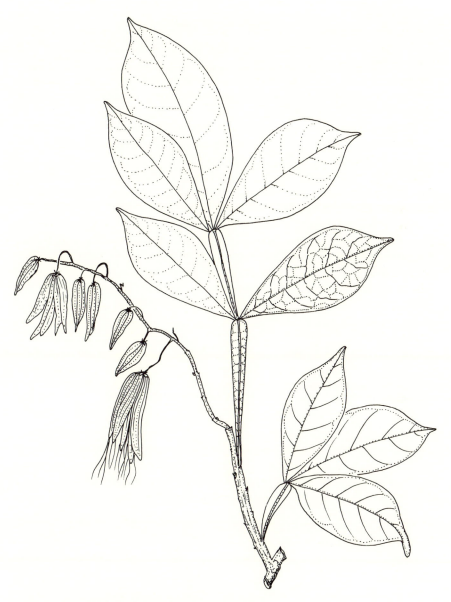

Figure 33. *Udud bungid.* (Enrique Tejada)

Obser, Dulup sigagid (*Zamia skinneri* Warsc. and *Z. cunaria* Dress. & Stev.) (Cycadaceae)

These two plants have leaves similar to those of palms. The leaves grow directly from the soil from a subterranean stem when the plants are young. The leaf blade is characteristically divided into leaflets or elongated, thin folioles. Generally, the leaf petiole has spines that look like lobster antennae. (*Dulup sigagid* means lobster antenna.) The fruit is a structure called a cone, which also grows directly from the soil. The cone contains bright red seeds, which sometimes turn brown. The seeds are naked.

Zamia skinneri is found in the forest to 1,000 meters. In Kuna Yala it is one of the plants that regenerates most rapidly on land that has been burned for planting.

Another species, *Z. cunaria*, was recently discovered in the Gangandi region. *Cunaria* refers to the Kuna. The species has yet to be found in any other part of tropical America.

This group of plants is preferred by Kuna doctors and herbalists to provoke vomiting. The subterranean stem is grated and cooked over a fire to obtain an extract that is administered in small quantities. The petiole and the leaves are also used in medicinal baths as a body purifier. The fruit is used to treat hemorrhoids in children. Figure 34 illustrates the habit of a plant of approximately one meter in height, with a fruit arising from the subterranean stem.

—Heraclio Herrera

Figure 34. *Dulup sigagid.* (Ologuagdi)

11

The *Ueruk* Palm

The tropical rain forest is a natural resource of vital importance to the human race. Its great plant and animal diversity has sustained—and continues to sustain—the development of many native cultures based on a complex and intimate relationship between plants and human beings.

Among the natural resources of the jungle, the palms stand out because of their abundance and their economic importance. They supply us with oil, starch, fiber, sugar, and alcohol. Palms are also important as a source of food, construction materials, medicines, and tools for domestic use. Furthermore, there has been considerable interest in the use of palms as an alternative to deforestation and as a way of preventing soil erosion.

The emphasis that we give to the *ueruk* palm is proportional to its value in the Comarca. Since the middle of the last century, *ueruk* is one of the palms whose leaves have been used to construct the roofs of thousands of Kuna dwellings because the leaves are inexpensive (ten to fifteen cents each).

The Kuna work expertly with the *ueruk*, a palm that offers the community a way to safeguard its valuable but fragile forests. As the culture and belief systems of indigenous peoples gradually deteriorate, knowledge and experience regarding the use of natural resources are also in danger of disappearing. Therefore, it is vital to pass on traditional knowledge regarding the use of the *ueruk* palm.

Botanical Aspects of the *Ueruk* Palm

Ueruk is a plant that, in botanical terms, belongs with the palms of the family Arecaceae, a group that includes, among others, *ogob* (coconut palm, *Cocos nucifera*), *nalub* (pixbae, *Bactris gasipaes*), *ila* (jira, *Socratea exorrhiza*), *irsu* (corneto, *Iriartea gigantea*), *soska* (guágara, *Cryosophila warscewiczii*), and *signugar* (caña brava, *Bactris* sp.).

Western botanists know *ueruk* by its scientific name, *Manicaria sac-cifera* Gaertn., given by the German botanist Joseph Gaertner, who collected the plant in South America at the end of the eighteenth century. "Manica" means "sleeve" in Latin, and "saccifera" means "burlap." The name describes the fibrous covering that encloses the infructescence.

Description

Ueruk has a tall, robust trunk, which is usually erect but may be twisted or grow at an angle. It grows as a solitary tree and also in groups (fig. 35).

Ordinarily, two stems arise from the base. Sometimes they divide a meter above the soil line. The trunk grows up to seven meters tall and displays scars of fallen leaves similar to the leaf scars on coconut palms. It also has a dense mass of roots at the base. Its leaves are large and up to eight meters long, with blades nearly two meters wide; they are either entire or divided. The flowers are found inside a fibrous sac. When the palm flower matures, the sac opens and the fruits fall. The fruits are large, round, and between three and seven centimeters in diameter. They may have from one to three lobes, depending on the number of seeds they contain. The husk of the fruit has spiny projections that are remnants of the flower stigmas.

Origin

Geographically, *ueruk* comes from Central America (Nicaragua), spans the Caribbean Sea (through Trinidad), and extends into the mainland again along the delta of the Orinoco River in Venezuela and the Guayanas, to the lower stretches of the Amazon River.

In Panama, *ueruk* is found in Bocas del Toro, Colón, in the Canal Area, and in the Kuna Comarca. In Kuna Yala it is found in its native state in Gangandi, Nusadup, Urgandi, Guebdi, Yanndup, Ukupa, Ukupseni, Dad Nakue Dupbir, Dubuala, and Carreto. Nusadup, Urgandi, Guebdi, and Ukupa have extensive stands of palms, which will supply leaves for roofing for many years. Plantations of *ueruk* exist only in Muladup, Dubuala, and Goedup. Efforts are being made to cultivate palms in other communities, as well.

Habitat

Ueruk grows on small knolls throughout freshwater swamps and swampy areas near the coast and may sometimes form dense stands. In Kuna Yala, adult palms from seven meters in height are found in areas that are

Figure 35. A *ueruk* palm eight meters tall and between thirty and forty years old. At left, on the trunk, hangs the fibrous sac that contains the fruit. At right is an inflorescence. (Ologuagdi)

flooded up to 1.4 meters deep in the rainy season. Evidently, *ueruk* is also tolerant to flooding with salt water.

The associated vegetation is composed of a coastal strip of mangroves (*Rhizophora mangle*), behind which *ueruk* grows among palms such as *sama ga* (*Elaeis oleifera*), and other plants such as *soila uala* (*Prioria copaifera*), *bupur* (*Montrichardia arborescens*), *durgab* (*Terminalia* sp.) and *esnargan* ferns (*Acrostichum aureum*). Farther from the coast it grows among *ueue* trees (*Pterocarpus officinalis*), *yambina* (*Amanoa guianensis*), and mango (*Mangifera indica*).

Uses

We are not certain about when the Kuna began to use the leaves of the *ueruk* palm in roof construction. Even before they began to migrate—driven by Spanish conquistadors and by other indigenous tribes—from the mainland areas that today are known as the provinces of Panamá and Darién, the Kuna were using the leaves of plants, presumably including palm leaves, as the roofs of their dwellings. In *Travel and Description of the Isthmus of Darién* (1699), chronicler Lionel Wafer indicates that the roofs of native dwellings were made of palm fronds.

According to the literature, the range of the *ueruk* palm extends from Central through South America, principally along the Atlantic coast. The Kuna may have begun to use the leaves of the *ueruk* as roofing material when they arrived near the coast in the last half of the nineteenth century. They also collected *ueruk* seeds and planted them, a practice that persists.

For the Kuna, plants are the material basis of life. And if there is a single part of life that involves the use of both great quantities of plant material and a diversity of plant species, it is the construction of homes. Various species of plants are used in the construction of roofs, walls, wall supports, beams, and lofts. Palm leaves—especially those of *ueruk*, *uannuk*, *soska*, *igua*, and *sama*—are preferred for the roof. Palm leaves can be folded in such a way that rainwater readily drains off. They are also thicker than the leaves of other plants, making them more durable (fig. 36).

Ueruk leaves are preferred in the islands of the Comarca, where it is said that they last for more than thirty years, depending on the quality of the construction. Ordinarily, when a dwelling is torn down to replace the structural supports, the roof of *ueruk* is reused for the new house.

The *uannuk* (*Welfia georgii*) is the next most commonly used roofing material in the mainland community of Gangandi. Today it is also being used more and more often on the islands. It is important to note that in the villages where *uannuk* is used more and more often, the Kuna must

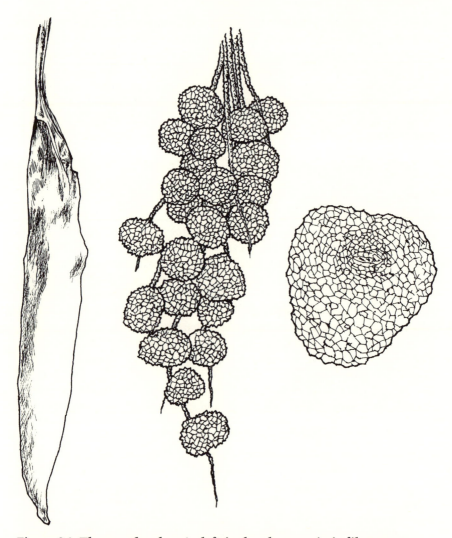

Figure 36. The *ueruk* palm: At left is the characteristic fibrous sac that contains the fruit, in the center, the infructescence, and at the right, a trilobate fruit. (Ologuagdi)

walk farther (up to three days) to virgin forests near the mountains to find leaves suitable for durable roofs.

The leaves of *uannuk* last only ten years in areas near the ocean because of their poor ability to tolerate the salty air. *Uannuk* is found in lowlands up to one thousand meters above sea level and generally grows farther inland than does *ueruk*.

Even though most of the palms used in construction are native to the Kuna region, only the *ueruk* is cultivated. We do not know of other attempts by the Kuna to cultivate palm species other than coconut palm, the pixbae, and the *ueruk*.

Today, the continued use of the *ueruk* palm is threatened because the number of trees has diminished notably as a result of overexploitation and the transformation into agricultural fields of the areas in which it was grown. The current number of *ueruk* is insufficient to satisfy the demands of Kuna communities.

The Kuna often use the bract, a fibrous bag-shaped structure that covers the fruit, to store cacao and tobacco seeds, to obtain fiber for the cords used to transport bananas, and for backpacks. Both adults and children wear the bract as a hat.

The *Ueruk* in Kuna Yala

Gardi

The region of Gardi includes all of the land and communities situated in the western part of the Comarca from Punta San Blas to the island of Miria Ubigandup. Here we found several adult stands of *ueruk* in 1986 and 1987. Although *ueruk* was used for roofing, the people of Gangandi preferred *uannuk* leaves. In Gardi, stands of *ueruk* came up in little patches, and in Miria Ubigandup some farmers carefully maintained a few groves.

According to the testimony of an *argar*, the Kuna in Mandi Ubigandup, a small island in the Gulf of San Blas, harvested native *ueruk* growing near the Mandi River in the 1940s. However, flooding of the Mandi River and its tributaries destroyed these stands. After this disaster, realizing that *ueruk* was indispensable for construction, *saila* Pipi dedicated himself to its cultivation. The *saila* was strongly criticized because he frequently traveled to other communities and to Colón to look for *ueruk* seeds, and many said that his efforts would be in vain. However, his farmlands were inherited by his sons and today several houses have been roofed with *ueruk* from his plantations.

Nusadup and Urgandi (Río Sidra)

This area includes in its jurisdiction the islands of Nusadup, Urgandi, and Mormakedup. *Ueruk* is not cultivated but it grows in dense stands sufficient to meet the needs of these communities. Farmers from other islands (Aridup, Ailidup, Orosdup, and Gardi) come to harvest *ueruk* leaves. Because the palm is abundant, the farmers do not value, and often eliminate, seedlings and the smallest palms around trees where they are harvesting leaves for roofing. In addition, they cut down some of the adults that reseed the area. There is a high density of *ueruk* seedlings and juveniles in flooded areas and on stream banks; nonetheless, adult stands of the palm are rare and the number of stumps is considerable.

Guebdi

The territory under the jurisdiction of the village of Guebdi (or Río Azúcar) is entirely on the mainland. Here, no one cultivates *ueruk* because of its abundance in the region extending to the Nuudiuar (Paloma) River. Inhabitants of other communities such as Gardi, Nurdup, Digir, Yanndup (Nargana), Akuanusadup (Corazón de Jesús), and Ukupseni come to find *ueruk* leaves for their roofs. Because so many farmers from other islands frequently entered the forest without the local *saila*'s permission, he eventually denied authorization for the harvest of *ueruk* and thus contributed to the conservation of the resource for the use of local residents. The *saila* confirms that people from other communities also come here to collect seeds.

Ukupa

The community of Ukupa (or Playón Grande) is situated on the coast of the mainland. It is a region that also has dense natural stands of *ueruk*, although its cultivation is practiced by a few farmers as well. In the neighboring community of Aidirgandi a farmer reportedly has a *ueruk* plantation, and in Irgandi, the farmers conserve and maintain fields of *ueruk* palm. Both villages sell *ueruk* leaves for ten cents each, and at times they still offer *ueruk* leaves and seeds to other communities at no cost.

Ukupseni

Before 1940, there were extensive mainland stands of *ueruk* near Ukupseni (Playón Chico). In a place called Ueruk Sukun (Bay of Ueruk), located one kilometer from the island, the palms were abundant under the leafy *ueue* trees.

During the same decade, the people began a project to cultivate coconut palms in areas where *ueruk* palms were growing. Large flooded areas were drained by digging channels and the *ueue* and *ueruk* trees were felled. Sites similar to Ueruk Sukun were also drained and cleared of palms for plantings of bananas, plantains, sugarcane, and corn. As a result, only isolated patches of *ueruk* have survived. Very few farmers dedicated themselves to the cultivation of *ueruk,* although others became responsible for the maintenance of natural stands of *ueruk.* These have since become their private property.

Dubuala (Tubuala) and Goedup

Although there were once isolated stands of *ueruk* in this area, these were carelessly exploited and became rare. The foresight and prompt action of Cacique Yabiliginya kept this resource from disappearing from his village. Today there are large plantations on private farmlands that produce leaves from 1.5 to 2 meters long, which are in high demand in the Comarca for use as roofing material.

Dubuala owes previous generations thanks for establishing the plantations that now exist. The children and grandchildren of these pioneer farmers have inherited these plantations and, in some cases, the same lands have been divided among several relatives. Now there are only a few wild *ueruk* plants, and nearly all of the leaves that are produced are from cultivated or managed trees.

Cultivation of the *Ueruk* Palm

The *saila* of Dubuala, Abelardo González, states that the

> *ueruk* palm is like a person: if it is in good health and in a pleasant environment, it grows fast and strong; and if the opposite is true, it will grow slowly, weaken, and finally die. A *ueruk* likes a lot of water, but water in excess will kill its shoots. Therefore, in cultivated areas we open quite a few drainage canals so that the water will drain off of the soil surface, leaving it damp and cool, the optimum condition for the *ueruk* to ensure that it grows rapidly.

The Seeds

The preferred way to grow *ueruk* is to begin with a germinated seed that has a root from one to ten centimeters long and a well-developed plumule (fig. 37). In Kuna, these seeds are called *musumusuguag.* The seeds are collected at the bases of tall trees, where they are piled under the decomposing palm leaf litter. The Kuna search for seeds at the bases of palm leaves; in cultivated *ueruk,* they use fruit that has naturally fallen to the ground.

The Kuna know which seeds are viable for cultivation by their darker color, when the branch that supports the fruit is angled toward the ground, and when the bract opens. Furthermore, they note that the fruit

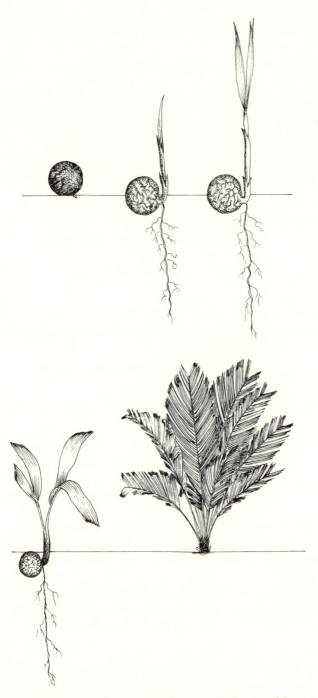

Figure 37. Stages of growth of a *ueruk* palm. (Ologuagdi)

has begun to fall onto the ground through the spaces among the leaves. The Kuna frequently collect small seedlings (up to forty centimeters in height), which they dig up with the surrounding soil and transplant immediately into cultivated areas.

After the seeds are collected, they are placed in containers in the shade and watered daily. Later the containers are taken home and placed on the ground in the bathing area, where they are frequently watered. The farmers in Dubuala often mix black earth with clayey soil as a substrate for germination. They dig up about ten centimeters of the soil in the yard or bathing area and fill in the hole with this mixture. Later, they place the germinating *ueruk* seeds on this bed and keep them damp until the leaves emerge. Others place this soil mixture in cups, plastic bags, or the husks of the *naba* fruit (*Crescentia cujete*).

Once the seeds have well-developed leaves, they are removed with the surrounding soil; care is taken not to damage the roots. To transplant the seedlings, the Kuna make a deep hole with a stick and place the plant so that its roots extend vertically into the soil.

When the fruit are mature, they are placed on the ground in mounds of soil under the leafy *ueue* trees. The husk of the fruit decomposes and then the seeds begin to germinate.

Cultivated Lands

Ueruk is preferably cultivated in land with rich or clayey soil under leafy trees, such as *ueue* or mango trees, frequently in flooded areas. We also find many cultivated palms on stream banks. A farmer told us that he had placed seeds on a stream bank and was surprised to find that the floods had not removed them, because nearly all of them germinated. Now they are five meters tall. Various plantations in Dubuala and several in Ukupseni are maintained between coconut groves in sandy areas in full sun.

Shaded plantations of *ueruk* are more successful because of the noticeable effect of natural light on the quality of leaves. In shade, the leaves are dark green, healthy and strong. In very sunny areas, such as the coconut groves, the *ueruk* leaves have reddish-purple spots, are more ragged (in part because of wind), and evidently are not as desirable as roofing material.

The Plantation

Plantations are maintained by constantly pruning wilted leaves (usually the outermost), cleaning away leaf litter around tree trunks, removing old trunks, and, above all, clearing the area around each tree. Wilted, shrunken, and fallen leaves as well as leaves that have become cracked or brittle are pruned from permanently established plants by cutting them at the base of the petiole and at the soil line.

The Kuna know that remnants of the petiole left on the plant trap a lot of trash and moisture that can damage the three or four remaining leaves. They also know that the litter provides favorable conditions for insects, scorpions, and termites to make their nests between the leaf bases and, subsequently, to damage the leaves.

Three- to five-year-old palms are pruned by cutting the petiole of damaged leaves; about twenty-five centimeters are left at the base. These petioles absorb excess moisture through the cut end and keep the plant cool; at the same time, they prevent the young inner leaves from rotting.

Pruning also involves removing the oldest trunks. These trunks have inaccessible leaves or leaves that are not a suitable size for use in construction. Their seeds have been planted and normally they have three to five sprouts of three meters or less joined at the base, so that the cut does not kill the plant.

When the trunk is cut, fruit that has fallen in clusters at the base is piled in a cleared area and covered with leaves from the trunk. When the seeds germinate they are transplanted to other sites. Occasionally, the fruit is left where it falls, but the Kuna know that some seeds will germinate, increasing the number of *ueruk* in their plantation.

A young farmer told us that he witnessed his grandfather maintaining his plantations with controlled burns. The farmer experimented by setting fire to the trunks of *ueruk* and to the outermost leaves, taking care not to burn the new leaf in the center. The fire destroys the husks of the fruit, permitting the seeds to germinate. Following this, one is certain to have a second generation of *ueruk* on the same site. Another farmer informed us that he had burned off the grass on a part of his plantation where he had cultivated seeds months before. Afterwards he noticed *ueruk* sprouting at the site.

Given that the seeds of *ueruk* are preyed on by agoutis, crabs, and some beetles, the Kuna protect them with sections of bamboo from two to three centimeters wide. The bamboo is trimmed to leave a point at one end and a tube at the other end. The sections are placed so that the tube forms a wall around the seed, with the point anchored in the soil. The bamboo is removed when the seed germinates and no longer fits under its cover.

In Dubuala, Belisario Porras, one of the surviving *ueruk* growers, cuts pieces of *caña blanca* (wild cane) thirty centimeters long, which he uses to fence off the seeds and young shoots of *ueruk* with a circle of cane that is approximately twenty centimeters in diameter. Each piece of cane is tied to the next with a cord.

Harvesting the Leaves

Leaf harvest—usually one week before putting a roof on a house—depends on the date set by the community for the collective construction of a house (fig. 38). These days, builders do not depend exclusively on the availability of *ueruk*, because they have the option of using other palms. When the harvest begins, first the outermost leaves are cut; the inner, more tender leaves are saved for later harvest. In most areas of Kuna Yala, natural stands of *ueruk* are young and the leaves are 1.5 meters long. The *ueruk* leaves from the plantations in Dubuala are 3 or more meters long. In this community the custom is to choose leaves that measure 2.5 arm lengths. This corresponds to roughly 2 meters, the required size for harvest. They choose leaves that are divided along the rachis. They stack the two parts and roll them up in order to tie them in a bundle.

To roof a standard house (8 meters by 5 meters) for a young couple, one needs approximately three thousand leaves, each 1.5 meters long, or the leaves of twenty to thirty *ueruk* trees up to twenty years old. Obviously, if the leaves are larger and are the right size for construction (2 meters), the number of leaves necessary is considerably reduced.

The Experience of Dubuala

Among the several communities that have tried to cultivate *ueruk* palm in the past, the island of Dubuala has been the most successful in this undertaking. It all began with Cacique Yabiliginya, well known for his leadership in the defense of the territory of Kuna Yala. Yabiliginya taught that one ought to take care of the earth and drive away the colonists who were settling the Comarca. To be able to subsist one must cultivate the *ueruk*, since he predicted a scarcity of leaves for roofing.

One night several dugout canoes carrying a group of Kuna set out over the sea to the mainland in search of *ueruk* seeds. At dawn the men entered the forest at different sites in the Dubuala region. Their work involved the harvest of thousands of seeds and their transport to several farms. The Kuna planted the seeds, dug drainage ditches in flooded areas, fenced in the seeds, and cleared plantation sites. They also planted seeds at the edges of coconut groves and near pineapple, banana, sugarcane, and cacao plantings. Plantations were established under *ueue* trees and others under mangoes. Today it is estimated that these plantings are between thirty and forty years old. Few of the pioneer farmers who cultivated *ueruk* are still alive. Their plantations were left as their legacy to their children and grandchildren.

—Heraclio Herrera

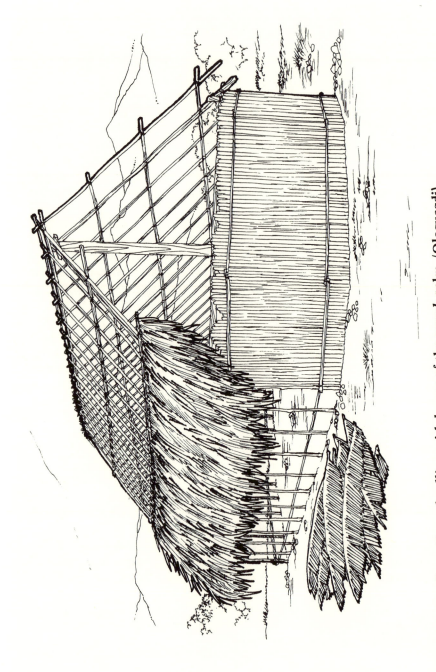

Figure 38. Roofing a Kuna dwelling with leaves of the *ueruk* palm. (Ologuagdi)

12

To Be or Not to Be

It has always been true that where there is Napguana, the earth, or Mother Nature, indigenous culture flourishes, but that it dies in her absence. The link between Napguana and the material life of the Olodulegan is an ontological matter, a matter of being, and not of meaning, because Napguana is the basis of the material and spiritual existence of the nations of Abya Yala. The communion of the Gungidule with Napguana is intimate and is formed in such a way that the border between spiritual Napguana and material Napguana is blurred. To better understand this "savage idea," it occurred to me that it could be illustrated by thinking of a photograph that, as we know, is composed of one negative part and one positive part, both in the developed and in the undeveloped state. The material essence is transformed into the spiritual essence in the same way. Napguana is synonymous with Nana, that is, Mother. Thus, the poet René of Gardi wrote:

Thus spoke the Saila of Gardi:

> There are those who have two wives,
> but all of us have only one mother.
> There are those who deal blows of steel to their wives,
> but we make the days of our mother delightful.
> There are those who witness the death of their woman,
> but mother outlives us all.
> There are those who, after becoming widowed, remarry,
> but one's mother is never widowed.
> There are those who have property and use it to cut deals,
> but no one would dream of prostituting his mother.
> There are those who betray their wives,
> but the good sons never betray their mother:
> their homeland.

The arrival of the Spanish marked the beginning of the downfall of Abya Yala, a disgrace in every sense of the word, because the Spanish brought only desolation and death. To say "Spanish" is synonymous with saying "all of our troubles taken together." No conqueror, Syrian, Roman or gringo (and I am not saying Greek, by mistake, but gringo), did more damage in demographic terms, or on the basis of their criminality and plundering, to one hundred million human beings nor pillaged the depths of the earth as assiduously as the Spanish did. They are responsible for the first ecocide in all of human history. Now, before the earth suffers more damage than it already has, it is imperative that we form alliances with all of the people of the world, to struggle hand in hand to try to stop the deterioration of the ecosystem.

These events demonstrate that we, the Gungidulegan, are guardians of nature not only at the level of discourse but also at the level of our actions. At this level we continue to feel the dynamic tradition, to feel respect for nature, because as Ailton Krenak, an indigenous man, a Brazilian, and a fighter for the rights of native peoples in the international forum, said: "We do not have to defend Nature, we have to respect her."

Respect for nature is part of the Kuna tradition. Nevertheless, it is necessary to make an observation: In the last few years, the Kuna Comarca of San Blas has been inundated with canned food and the people toss the containers into the sea, polluting it. Therefore, in light of this situation, in light of this unpublicized situation, it is necessary to educate them about the environment. In the schools of San Blas, Spanish classes should be replaced by classes in ecology; to us it is more vital.

In general, the youth of today, and the people whom they will become, are the most alienated in the world. I do not want to say that there are no exceptions. The truth is that today we are beginning to see more clearly the products of an explosion of western alienation that has arrived with the force of an electrical storm and that has mortally wounded Dule identity. Nonetheless, unfortunately, the Gungidulegan, in the manner of demagogues, have been able to successfully sell to the outside world the image of being the most Indian of the Indians. There is no doubt that they are the most astute Indians!

There is no question that the Gungidulegan had a splendid history, a majestic history. But that is something that belongs to the past. We are not the protagonists of our history. Those who sell our image today as if we were still the same people we were in the good old days do it as mystification or as romanticism or in bad faith or simply because they are afraid to confront reality. "How many birds nest in their idle heads!"

Frequently, the Gungidulegan echo the words of Cacique Yabiliginya: "Who says that we are tired of being Indians?" Had there not been the slightest suspicion of such a weakness, he would not have asked such a question. The official culture of Panama, that is, Ladino culture, struck a lethal blow to the Dulepanamanian culture by attacking, first, the language, which the Ladinos call "dialect," and then mathematics.

In the private schools in Panama City, French and English are taught in addition to Spanish. Meanwhile, in the public schools of San Blas, the "little Indian" is prohibited from using the mother tongue and is obliged to replace it with Spanish. In other words, while the middle- and upper-class children in the cities learn, beginning in first grade, two additional languages as well as perfecting the use of their mother tongue, the poor "little Indian" goes to school to be deculturated. The Indian child unlearns the native tongue and begins to chatter in the dialect of Vulgar Latin that is Spanish. The Ministry of Education is in complicity with other decadent types, who say: "Why should the Gungidule learn to speak Dule if he already does?"

Why, then, do Ibero-American universities have Spanish departments, if Spanish is the native tongue of the Ladinos? When do we ever see a French or English person linguistically castrating his child? The first class to abandon its language is the bourgeoisie and among the Kuna, the self-baptized "intellectuals."

The cultural minorities have not lost everything; at least we can be consoled in the case of Catalonian. To arrive in Catalonia is to arrive in a community that has overcome Spanish tyranny and that reappears today, born anew and full of love for life. In the streets you no longer hear Spanish spoken. The children speak Catalonian in school, as God commands. A degree in Catalonian philology from the University of Barcelona is held in higher regard than a degree in Spanish philology. This is how it ought to be. "The language is not merely a means for expressing a thought," said the English mathematician Boole, "rather it is a tool of human reason."

In terms of mathematics, the Kuna situation is equally infuriating. To count in Dulegaya, it is necessary to master arithmetic, geometry, and fundamental concepts. Number, form, and calculation configure the counting system in Dulegaya. This explains why money and fish are not counted in the same way.

We see that—

11 = (10 + 1), i.e., one must add.

80 = (20 x 4), i.e., one must multiply.

90 = (20 x 4 + 10), one must multiply and add.

With the system of counting in Spanish, how many future Galileos, Descartes, Fermats, Pascals, Laplaces, Poincarés, Cantors . . . have been poisoned in the schools of San Blas?

My generation, who are between thirty-five and fifty years old, is the last generation of the Gungidulegan, since the future belongs to those who elect to live: The Kuna have opted to commit suicide.

Within the dialectic of colonialism, there is no middle ground: a place is colonized or not colonized. In good Spanish, María Moliner, who confuses Mexico with Cuzco, translates the term "cholo" as "civilized Indian," in other words, as having been colonized. Haven't we seen the same Indians giving rise to "the Father of Civilization in San Blas" or "the Day of Civilization" or the "Park of Civilization"? Poor dears! What comedians! In truth, I say: colonization and "cholonization" are one and the same!

Nietzsche said that the Jews were a unique group of people in world history because, when faced with the dilemma of whether "to be or not to be," with cold determination, they decided "to be," at whatever price. But the Kuna have chosen the easiest route: suicide. By Nietzschean reckoning, "the banker immediately thinks about business, the Christian about sin, and the girl about her love." I will add one further thought: "and the Kuna about 'cholonization.'" When the *saila* of Gardi thinks that the beasts are able to worsen our ecosystem more, the youngster, on his part, is thinking about who is going to be the next beast who is coming to present his next erotic salsa show. . . . I hope to God that the prophetic words of Nostradamus do not come true: "From the sidereal archipelago the men of the golden race respond in unison to the west."

—Arysteides Turpana, Dule poet
Kingston–Machu Picchu (April–June 1992)
(Recorded by Valerio Núñez)

Epilogue

In 1967 I was a Peace Corps volunteer stationed at the Mandinga Agricultural School in the Gardi region. The school was situated on the mainland about a half hour's journey upriver from the Bay of Moliyaa on a flat, poorly drained tract of land adjacent to a series of heavily wooded foothills. Over a period of two years, we spent most of our time in the forest, clearing land, planting crops, fighting back the ever-advancing wall of vegetation, or simply wandering about exploring. We passed our weekends on the islands.

At the time, I was greatly impressed by the profusion of both marine and terrestrial animals in the Gardi area, which contains the most abundant sea life in San Blas. The water surrounding the numerous coral islands is generally shallow, characterized by wide expanses of sea grass pastures and coral reefs, and it extends far out to encompass the barrier islands of Kaimau. On the islands of Nalunega and Wichubuala, near the far western point of the Comarca, I sometimes came across trussed-up turtles lying on their backs on the sandy beaches, together with the wooden decoys and tangled nets used to entrap them. In July and August, the men returned from nighttime expeditions with boatloads of large tarpon speared as they migrated west along the irregular contours of the coast. Throughout the outer reefs, with their labyrinths of canals and caves interlaced through the coral, there were schools of fish, lobsters, crabs, sharks, and occasional turtles. Seafood was always present on the menu, often in abundance.

On the mainland, multitudes of green iguanas lived in the upper branches of trees in a vast shallow swamp extending inland a short distance from the school. Farther inland, white-lipped peccaries traveling in packs were frequent pillagers of Kuna farms, rooting up manioc and tearing apart cornfields. The forest in this area, to the north of the village of Gangandi, was thick and it was populated by monkeys of various sorts, white-lipped and collared peccaries, agoutis, pacas, curassows, guans, chachalacas, parrots, and toucans.

I do not want to give the impression that during this period we were stumbling over animals every time we ventured into the forest; game animals in tropical forests are always sparse, even in the best of conditions. But the game was there; the students had stories of spotting jaguars and other cats during evening forays, tapir tracks were often found in the soft mud near the stream running past the school, and from time to time we were assaulted by the powerful musk of collared peccary as we penetrated the vegetation directly behind the school buildings.

I was unaware at that time that the abundance I saw about me was already in sharp decline and was thus to a large extent illusory. In fact, the Kuna were standing at the tail end of a process of unsustainable use of the resource base that had been unfolding, inexorably, for decades. For in the late 1960s there was talk of the disappearance of the turtles and the schools of tarpon from the sea; there was a growing shortage of *ueruk* thatch and timber for construction and, in many areas, good firewood; hunters were finding it necessary to pursue their prey deeper and deeper into the forest. There were indications that things were going badly, hints here and there, but the situation was not yet visibly critical, and most of us simply chose to ignore it.

Today the signs are unmistakable as we see stretching out before us an increasingly barren landscape. Turtles are rarely seen, much less caught; the wooden decoys and tanglenets that were so common a few years back no longer litter Kuna patios. Lobsters are on the verge of extinction, and the few that are now caught all find their way into the hands of foreign buyers rather than the *dule masi*. The coral reefs are dying and the schools of fish are vanishing. The large seasonal runs of tarpon have become nothing more than memories in the minds of older villagers, and the weirs once built to catch them have broken apart and collapsed. Many of the islands are surrounded by growing fields of discarded cans, plastic containers, and broken remnants of Western civilization. Game animals are becoming rarer and rarer along the mainland coastal strip. Men must travel farther and farther to find certain kinds of plants and wood for construction.

This disturbing picture has been taking form in a context of rapid and disorienting change in Kuna society. Western education has spread to even the most remote corners of the Comarca since it penetrated the region in the early years of this century. The population has been growing exponentially over the last few decades, creating pressures for physical space in the communities and for agricultural land. Especially since the 1960s, numerous Kuna have migrated to Panama City and Colón for education and work. There is now a constant flow of people and ideas back and forth between San Blas and Panama.

Money and commercial goods have become an increasingly important part of this flow, to the point where the cash economy plays a dominant role in Kuna life. Fundamental values have changed. In many areas of San Blas, the exchange of money has supplanted the traditional value of hospitality and sharing. Fishing and hunting, once strictly subsistence activities, are now undertaken for the money they will bring. The teachings of Pab Igala, the chant tradition of the "Gathering" (*onmakket*), carry a strong conservationist message that is often ignored by the younger generations of Kuna. Even the physical disappearance of species that were once an important part of Kuna life is not sufficiently jolting to make people change their ways.

The difficulties faced by the Kuna are by no means unique; they are part of a pattern found all along the Caribbean slope of Central America. It is in this region that the few remaining forests remain, and it is here that the indigenous societies of Central America have a strong presence: more than twenty ethnic/linguistic groups, stretching from Belize through Panama to the Colombian border, have been living in and taking care of these forests for thousands of years. It is here that we find the greatest density of both biological and cultural diversity.

Until recently, these groups lived in isolation, in regions of refuge, largely protected from the incursions of the outside world by the thick stands of forest, the heavy rainfall, and the generally inhospitable (to outsiders) environment. Now all of this has changed. Since the 1940s, exponential population growth throughout Central America (from 1940 to 1990, the population tripled, reaching twenty-five million), capitalist schemes utilizing new technologies, and advances in public health have combined to open these areas up to exploitation by loggers, cattle ranchers, and swarms of landless peasants. Multinational companies are extending their tentacles into the last remaining hinterlands in search of cheap timber and oil and precious minerals. As all of these forces advance, the forests are being cut down and burned off at a steadily accelerating pace, and the native inhabitants are deprived of their resources, displaced, and driven into cultural extinction.

The physical arrival of these outsiders is bad enough; equally harmful, yet perhaps even more dangerous, are the values the West is exporting wholesale into the remaining indigenous areas of the region. Today's consumer society increasingly places a price tag on things that traditional societies have treated with respect and moderation. We on the outside are converting seemingly everything within our radius into a commodity, something that can be bought and sold on the market. Lobsters, turtles, game from the forest, trees, land—all become a source of income, of cash. Cacique Carlos López decries the penetration of these values and the loss of tradition and consensus thinking in San Blas. "There no longer exists the custom of acting together," he says. "Before, when a decision was made on a particular matter, everyone obeyed as a group. Today, they obey money. We are acquiring the soul of the *uaga*."

What is difficult to understand is the arrogance of Western society, which proclaims the superiority of a value system based on unsustainable resource use and which is contributing, as time marches forward at an ever quickening gait, to the destruction of the ecological balance of the entire planet. Even more difficult to understand is the seductive power of this value system. As if motivated by some form of insidious black magic, many of the indigenous peoples of the world are discarding their knowledge of the natural world, losing the underpinnings of traditional belief systems that promote respect for all living things, and buying into Western notions of "modernity" and "progress." They are acquiring the soul of the *uaga*.

This should not and need not be the case. Kuna society has managed to persist through centuries of adversity, and it remains resilient. The present collection of essays and testimonials is evidence of this resiliency. This collection is a sensitive and intelligent look at the ecological crisis—which, the authors make abundantly clear, is also a crisis of the spirit—facing the Kuna. But this is not merely a book for the Kuna. It is a grain-of-sand look at a crisis that is facing all of us and that must be overcome, cultural group by cultural group, if we are to survive on this planet.

The book is several things at once: a celebration, a lament, an introspective rumination, and a call for restoration of the ecological and spiritual balance. It is a celebration of the forest and the sea and a number of its creatures and plants in San Blas, and of the Kuna people, their culture, and their way of life. It is a lament for the erosion of cultural values, the depletion of the earth's resources, and the seeming inability of the Kuna people to put a stop to the despoilment of their natural patrimony.

It is an introspective look because while the authors, young and old alike, find many of the root causes of the ecological crisis emanating from beyond the boundaries of the Comarca, they see themselves as perpetuating and deepening the crisis: It is the Kuna who continue to steal eggs from the dwindling numbers of turtles intent on reproducing; it is the Kuna who loot the coral reefs with their spear guns and turn them into submarine deserts; it is the Kuna who are neglecting their traditional responsiblilities of caring for the Mother and all of her creatures. The implication of this conclusion, quietly yet persistently stated, is that at this particular time in their history, the Kuna, and only the Kuna, have in their hands the power to restore the balance to their small corner of the world.

None of this will be easy. The enormity of the task should never be underestimated, and the authors of the present volume are not glib about the prospects for change in a positive direction. But if any people, among all of the indigenous groups in Central America, have a chance of coming to terms with their spiritual self and regaining control of their behavior, these would appear to be the Kuna.

—Mac Chapin
Center for the Support of Native Lands
Arlington, Va.

Appendix A

Scientific and Vernacular Names of Plants and Animals

Mammals

Kuna Vernacular Name	English Vernacular Name	Scientific Name
Achu barbad	Jaguar	Panthera onca
Achu ginnid	Puma	Felis concolor
Ari	Iguana	Iguana iguana
Bero	Sloth	Bradypus infuscatus
Dede	Armadillo	Dasypus novencinctus
Goe	Red Brocket deer	Mazama americana
Goe bebe nikad, Uasar	White-tailed deer	Odocoileus virginianus
Guigib	Anteater	Tamandua mexicana
Moli	Tapir	Tapirus bairdii
Sugachu	Raccoon	Procyon lotor
Sule, Napanono	Paca	Cuniculus paca
Sur ginnid	Red spider monkey	Ateles geoffroyi
Sur uega	Capuchin monkey	Cebus capucinus
Uasar, Goe bebe nikad	White-tailed deer	Odocoileus virginianus
Uedar	Collared peccary	Tayassu tajacu
Usu	Agouti	Dasyprocta punctata
Yannu	White-lipped peccary	Tayassu pecari

Birds

Kuna Vernacular Name	English Vernacular Name	Scientific Name
Bakaka	Red-throated Caracara	Daptrius americanus
Cuama	Chachalaca	Penelope purpurascens
Gig	Gull	
Guiblo	Hawk	
Sigli	Crested guan	Crax rubra

Reptiles

Kuna Vernacular Name	English Vernacular Name	Scientific Name
Ari	Iguana	Iguana iguana
Morro	Green sea turtle	Chelonia mydas
Yauk	Hawksbill turtle	Eretmochelys imbricata

Plants

Kuna Vernacular Name	English Vernacular Name	Scientific Name
Abior		Dieffenbachia pittieri
Aili ginnid	Red mangrove	Rhizophora mangle
Asue	Avocado	Persea americana
Bachar	Piper	Piper culebranum; Pothomorphe peltata
Beno		Pachira aquatica
Biseb		Ocimum basilicum
Bunur		Calathea sp.

Plants, cont.

Kuna Vernacular Name	English Vernacular Name	Scientific Name
Bupur		Montrichardia arborescens
Demar ob	Sargasso grass	Sargassum sp.
Dilla		Triplaris cumingiana
Dingugia		Neurolaena lobata
Dior nugargid		Cyathea petiolata
Dubsangid		Aristolochia pfeiferi
Dulup sigagid		Zamia skinneri and Z. cunaria
Dupuar, Dupu		Gustavia superba
Durgab		Terminalia sp.
Esnargan		Acrostichum aureum
Gabi	Coffee	Coffea sp.
Gabur	Hot pepper	Capsicum sp.
Gannir iko		Randia aculeata
Gay	Sugarcane	Saccharum officinarum
Guabeu		Malouetia isthmica
Guandulu		Pentagonia wendlandii
Gugdar		Xanthosoma robustum
Guiba		Jatropha curcas
Gurgur sapi		Himatanthus articulatus
Igua		Attalea allenii
Igua		Dipteryx panamensis
Iko nasi		Randia aculeata
Ila		Socratea exorrhiza
Ina gaibid		Simaba cedron
Ina gaibid		Neurolaena lobata
Inaguag		Sapindus saponaria

Plants, cont.

Kuna Vernacular Name	English Vernacular Name	Scientific Name
Irsu		*Iriartea gigantea*
Isberuala		*Manilkara bidentata*
Mama	Manioc	*Manihot esculenta*
Mammar dubaled		*Philodendron brevispathum*
Mango	Mango	*Mangifera indica*
Mas-sunnad	Plantain	*Musa paradisiaca*
Masar	Wild cane	*Gynerium sagitatum*
Masi	Banana	*Musa sapientum*
Morgauk		*Sapindus saponaria*
Musguar		*Protium sp.*
Naba	Squash	*Crescentia cujete*
Naibe ugia		*Tectaria vivipara*
Naibe uar		*Dracontium dressleri*
Nalub		*Bactris gasipaes*
Nidirbi sakangid		*Anthurium ochranthum; A. subsignatum*
Oba	Corn	*Zea mays*
Obser		*Zamia skinneri* and *cunaria*
Ogob	Coconut	*Cocos nucifera*
Oluka dubaled		*Clidemia epiphytica*
Oros	Rice	*Oryza sativa*
Oros ginnid		*Oryza rufipogon*
Osi	Pineapple	*Ananas comosus*
Sama		*Elaeis oleifera*
Sia	Cacao	*Theobroma cacao*
Signugar		*Bactris sp.*
Soila uala		*Prioria copaifera*
Soska		*Cryosophila warscewiczii*
Sua		*Spondias mombin*

Plants, cont.

Kuna Vernacular Name	English Vernacular Name	Scientific Name
Surmas		Campsoneura sprucci
Suu	Fig	Ficus sp.
Uaa	Royal palm	Roystonia regia
Udud bungid		Quassia amara
Ueue		Pterocarpus officinalis
Uannuk		Welfia georgii
Ueruer sorbi dubgid		Gurania makoyana
Ueruk		Manicaria saccifera
Yambina		Amanoa sp.

Invertebrates

Kuna Vernacular Name	English Vernacular Name	Scientific Name
Angi	Spotted lobster	Panulirus guttatus
Dulup	Common, or spiny, Lobster	Panulirus argus
Dulup Arad	Green Lobster	Panulirus laevicauda
Uisi		Parribacus sp.
Uisi		Scyllarides aequinoctialis Panulirus gracillis

Fish

Kuna Vernacular Name	English Vernacular Name	Scientific Name
Mila	Tarpon	Megalops atlanticus

Appendix B

Kuna Communities

Some communities in the Comarca have more than one name. We use the names preferred by the Kuna, but we list the communities here that have other, commonly used names.

Preferred Name	Other Names
Ailigandi	Ailigandí
Akuanusadup	Corazón de Jesús
Armila	Armir, Armadi
Dad Nakue Dupbir	San Ignacio de Tupile
Dubuala	Tubualá
Galed	Carreto
Gangandi	Cangandi
Gardi (a region that includes a number of communities)	Cartí
Gardi Sugdup	Cartí Sugdup
Guebdi	Río Azucar
Madungandi	Bayano
Mandi	Mandinga
Mormaquedup	Isla Máquina
Muladup	Mulatupo
Narasgandup	Naranjo
Niadup	Niatuppu, Digandiki, Tikantikki
Ogobsukun	Concepción
Ukupa	Playón Grande
Ukupseni	Playón Chico
Usdup	Ustupo
Yanndup	Narganá

Glossary

Dulegaya is not written the same way by all of the Kuna or by non-Kuna who have studied their culture. For example, the letters "b," "c," "t," and "w" may also be written "p," "k," "d," and "v," respectively. We have made an effort to be consistent in terms of spelling, but we are aware that there may be other, equally valid criteria and words that have more appropriate spellings.

A
absoged—singer-guide, assistant to the *nele*
Abya Yala—America
aila—attic or loft
akua biski—coral reefs
akwanusagana—medicinal stones
argar—adviser and interpreter of the *saila*
argar dummad—chief adviser or interpreter, i.e., chief *argar*

B
Bab Dummad—Great Father, the Creator
Bab Igala—Treatise on the Great Father (Kuna Bible)
baba—father
Biseb Igar—treatment; chant to improve the intelligence (of hunters); chant for falling in love
boni—sickness
bundor ina—medicine for pregnancy or labor. Also called **muu ina**
burba—essential spirit, force, vigor

C
chicha (Spanish)—puberty ceremony

D
Dad Ibe. See **Ibeler**

dad nakue burua—wind from the northeast
dii burua—winds that bring rain
dubsangid—"vine that looks like cotton"
Dule—Kuna person, or the Kuna people
dule masi—traditional Kuna diet
dulegaya—Kuna language
Dule Nega—Kuna house, Kuna Yala
dulup burui—young lobsters
dulup galu—large "corrals" for lobsters awaiting sale

G
ga—leaf
galu (galumar, pl.)—sacred site (one that should not be altered)
-gan—one of several suffixes that indicate the plural, for example, **dulegan**
gandur (gandurgan, pl.)—chanter who presides at the puberty ceremony (the **chicha**)
goebipi—little child; fawn
giblo—hawk
gungidule—Kuna "man of gold"

I
Ibeler—Kuna prophet who was transformed into the sun. Also called **Dad Ibe**
Ibeorgun—Kuna prophet, ancestor of the modern Kuna
ibya ina—ophthalmologic medicine
igar obured—treatment of psychological problems
ina—plants used in traditional Kuna medicine
inaduled (inadulegan, pl.)—traditional Kuna doctor
ina burui—medicine for minor aches and pains
inna—*chicha* corn-based drink
inna suid—*chicha* (four days), female puberty ceremony

M
magad burua—gentle winds from the northeast
Mandi burua—winds from the west, "from the Mandi River"
mergi—people from the United States
mergi serred—in Gangandi, forest in the abandoned banana plantation
mola—fabric
morra—women's blouse
musumusuguag—*ueruk* palm seedlings
mutu sichid—black patch of sperm on female lobsters

muu ina—medicine for pregnancy or labor. Also called **bundor ina**

N
naibe—snake
naibe dugologuad—poisonous snake
nainu—cultivated area
nainu maduled—weedy pastureland
nainumar—plural of *nainu*
nainu nuchukua—young secondary forest
nainu serred—old secondary forest
nana—mother
Nan Dummad—Great Mother, wife of Bab dummad
Nan Gabsus—Mother of the Night, lit. "Mother sleep-brought"
Napguana—Mother Earth
naras—oranges and other citrus fruits
neg nuchukua—young secondary forest, lit. "young place"
neg serred—primary forest, lit. "old place"
nele (nelegan, pl.)—traditional doctor, shaman
nia ina—epilepsy treatment
Ninied Igar—the song about the birth of the marine turtle
nuchu—wooden statue, totem

O
ogob—coconut
Olodualigipileler—mythological name of the moon; father of Ibeler
Olodulegan—the Dule people, the Kuna; the "Golden People"
Onmaked Nega—Congress House
onmakket—the "Gathering"
orwaip—fish (from English, "old wife")

S
Sagir burua—winds from the Chagres River
saila dummagan—regional leaders, *caciques*
saila (sailagan, pl.)—person with highest authority in the community, chief
sibeb—beetle
suga—crab
surba—ceremonial enclosure for women

U
uaga (uagmala, pl.)—ladino, stranger, Spaniard, outsider
Uago—first man after the creation

uaymadun—banana variety
ulachui—dugout canoe
Ueruk Sukun—bay where the *ueruk* grow
usu yae—Dance of the Agouti

Y
yala burua—south winds, "from the mountains"
yalatela—fish (from the English "yellow tail")
yar suit—the "long land"
yolep—corn planting on the fertile banks of some large rivers in November and December
yoor burua—winds from the north, "winds of summer"

Bibliography

Anderson, Anthony B.
    1990   "Deforestation in Amazonia: Dynamics, Causes and Alterna-
              tives." In *Alternatives to Deforestation: Steps toward Sustain-
              able Use of the Amazon Rain Forest*, ed. Anthony B. Ander-
              son, pp. 1–23. New York: Colombia University Press.
Anderson, Anthony B., Peter H. May, and Michael J. Balick
    1988   *The Subsidy from Nature: Palm Forests, Peasantry, and
              Development on an Amazon Frontier*. New York: Colombia
              University Press.
Armuelles Boutet, R. A.
    1969   "La zonificación agrícola de Panamá." MA thesis. Instituto
              Interamericano de Ciencias Agrícolas (IICA), Turialba, Costa
              Rica. (Cited in Castillo y Beer, 1983.)
Atlas Nacional de la República de Panamá
    1988   *Instituto Geográfico Nacional "Tommy Guardia."* 3d ed.
Balick, Michael J.
    1986   *The Palm-Tree of Life: Biology, Utilization and Conservation.*
              Advances in Economic Botany, vol. 6. New York: New York
              Botanical Garden.
Barringer, Kerry
    1983   "Notes on Central American Aristolochiaceae." *Brittonia* 35,
              no. 2:171–174.
Castillo, Arcadio
    1992   "Análisis de la pesca actual de langosta espinosa (*Panulirus
              argus*) y otras langostas en Kuna Yala, Panamá." Technical
              report of the Office of Education. Panama City: Smithsonian
              Tropical Research Institute. Mimeo.
Castillo, Geodisio, and John W. Beer
    1983   "Utilización del bosque y de sistemas agroforestales en la
              Región de Gardi, Kuna Yala (San Blas, Panamá)." Turrialba,
              Costa Rica: Centro Agronómico Tropical de Investigación y
              Enseñanza (CATIE).
Chapin, MacPherson
    1975   "Kuna Subsistence. Comments and Addendum to: Notes on
              the Environment and Subsistence Practices of the San Blas

Cuna." Working Papers on Peoples of Central America, no. 1, pp. 53–60. Unpublished manuscript.

1982   "Memo on Udirbi Project." Roslyn, Va.: Inter-American Foundation. (Cited in Houseal et al., 1985.)

1983   "Curing among the San Blas Kuna of Panama." PhD dissertation. University of Arizona.

1989   *Pab Igala: Historias de la tradición Kuna*. Colección 500 Años, no. 5. Quito, Ecuador: Ediciones Abya-Yala; Rome: Movimiento Laicos para América Latina; Cayambe, Ecuador: Talleres Gráficos Abya-Yala.

1990   "Recapturing the Old Ways: Traditional Knowledge and Western Science Among the Kuna of Panama." Unpublished.

Charnley, Susan

1985   "Mamíferos del área del Proyecto PEMASKY." In *Informe de la caracterización ecológica del área del Proyecto PEMASKY*. Panama: Smithsonian Tropical Research Institute.

Charnley, Susan, and Cebaldo De León

N.d.   "Uso de recursos naturales en Kuna Yala occidental." Avance de Informe presentado al Proyecto PEMASKY. Panama.

Chiari, Aurelio

1977   "Nombres geográficos de la Comarca de San Blas." Bachelor's thesis. University of Panama.

Croat, Thomas

1978   *Flora of Barro Colorado Island*. Stanford, Calif.: Stanford University Press.

1986   *A Revision of the Genus* Anthurium (Araceae) *of Mexico and Central America. Part II: Panama*. Monographs in Systematic Botany, vol. 14. Missouri Botanical Garden. Saint Louis.

D'Arcy, William G.

1987   *Flora of Panama. Checklist and Index*. Parts I and II. Missouri Botanical Garden. St. Louis.

Denevan, William M. (ed.)

1976   *The Native Population of the Americas in 1492*. Madison: University of Wisconsin Press.

de Nevers, Greg, and Heraclio Herrera

1985   "Proyecto Botánico de PEMASKY/STRI: Informe Final." In *Informe de la caracterización ecológica del área del Proyecto PEMASKY*. Panama: Smithsonian Tropical Research Institute.

DeVries, Philip J.

1983   "*Zamia skinneri* and *Z. fairchildiana*." In *Costa Rican Natural History*, ed. Daniel H. Janzen, pp. 349–350. Chicago: University of Chicago Press.

Handley, Charles O.

1966   "Checklist of the Mammals of Panama." In *Ectoparasites of Panama*, ed. R. L. Wenzeland and V. Tipton, pp. 753–795. Chicago: Field Museum of Natural History.

Hasbrouck, Gary M.

1985   "Subsistence Fishing among the San Blas Kuna, Panama." MA thesis. University of California, Berkeley.

Herlihy, Peter
1986   "A Cultural Geography of the Embera and Wounaan (Chocó) Indians of Darién, Panama, with Emphasis on Recent Village Formation and Economic Diversification." PhD dissertation, Louisiana State University.
1989   "Panama's Quiet Revolution: Comarca Homelands and Indian Rights." *Cultural Survival Quarterly* 13, no. 3: 17–24.

Herrera, Francisco
1984   "La Revolución de Tule, Antecedentes y nuevos aportes." Bachelor's thesis, University of Panama.

Herrera, Heraclio
1991   "Plantas usadas en la medicina tradicional en el oeste de Kuna Yala (San Blas), Panamá." Bachelor's thesis. University of Panama.

Holdridge, Leslie, and Luis Poveda
1975   *Arboles de Costa Rica*. San José, Costa Rica: Centro Científico Tropical.

Holdridge, L.; W. Grenke; W. Hatheway; T. Liang; and J. Tosi, Jr.
1971   Forest Environments in Tropical Life Zones. New York Pergamon Press.

Holloman, Regina
1969   "Developmental Change in San Blas." PhD dissertation. Northwestern University.

Houseal, Brian; Craig MacFarland; Guillermo Archibold; and Aurelio Chiari
1985   "Indigenous Cultures and Protected Areas in Central America." *Cultural Survival 9*, no. 1: 10–20.

Howe, James
1974   "Village Political Organization among the San Blas Cuna." PhD dissertation. University of Pennsylvania.
1975   "Notes on the Environment and Subsistence Practices of the San Blas Cuna." Working Papers on Peoples of Central America, no. 1, pp. 1–53. Unpublished manuscript.
1980   *Cantos y oraciones del Congreso Cuna*. Panama: Editorial Universitaria.
1986   *The Kuna Gathering: Contemporary Village Politics in Panama*. Latin American Monographs, no. 67. Austin: University of Texas Press.

Ibelele, Olowahíppilele
1989   "Kuna Nihi Carta (Calendario Kuna para 1989)." Cartí Suidup: Academia de la Lengua Kuna. Mimeo.

Janzen, Daniel H.
1983   "*Odocoileus virginianus*." In *Costa Rican Natural History*, ed. Daniel H. Janzen, pp. 481–483. Chicago: University of Chicago Press.

Koford, C. B.
1983   "*Felis wiedii*." In Costa Rica Natural History, ed. Daniel H. Janzen, pp. 471–472. Chicago: University of Chicago Press.

Linares, Olga
1976 "Garden Hunting in the American Tropics." *Human Ecology* 4 (4): 331–349.

Méndez, Eustorgio
1970 *Los principales mamíferos silvestres de Panamá*. Panama: Imprenta Bárcenas

Morton, Julia
1981 *Atlas of Medicinal Plants of Middle America: Bahamas to Yucatan*. Springfield: Charles C. Thomas.

Nietschmann, Bernard
1971 "The Substance of Subsistence." In *Geographic Research on Latin America*. Proceedings, Conference of Latin Americanist Geographers, Muncie, Indiana, pp. 167–181.
1973 *Between Land and Water: The Subsistence Ecology of the Miskito Indians in Eastern Nicaragua*. New York: Seminar Press.

Nordenskiöld, Erland
1938 *An Historical and Ethnological Survey of the Cuna Indians*. Comparative Ethnographical Studies, no. 10. Goteborg, Switzerland: Goteborgs Museum, Etnografiska Avdelningen.

Orr, Katherine S.
1985 "La vida de la langosta espinosa." Washington, D.C.: World Wildlife Fund.

PEMASKY
1990 Comarca de la biósfera de Kuna Yala: Plan General de manejo y desarrollo (resúmen ejecutivo).

Peralta, Rodolfo; Rutilio Paredes; and Heraclio Herrera
1987 "Zonas de vida y descripción fisonómica de los bosques en el área de estudio del Proyecto PEMASKY." Panama: Informe de Consultoría del Centro Científico Tropical.

Porter, J. W.
1972 "Ecology and Species Diversity of Coral Reefs on Opposite Sides of the Isthmus of Panama." *Bol. Biol. Soc.*, no. 2: 88–116.

Prestán, Arnulfo
1975 *El uso de la chicha y la sociedad kuna*. Ediciones Especiales, no. 72. Mexico City: Instituto Indigenista Interamericano.

Restrepo, Vicente
1960 "Viajes de Lionel Wafer al Istmo del Darién (cuatro meses entre los indios)." *Revista Loteria*, no. 14. Trans. of *A New Voyage and Description of the Isthmus of America*, 1699.

Ribeiro, Darcy
1976 Configuraciones Histórico culturales americanas. 2d ed. Buenos Aires: Editorial Calicanto.

Roig y Mesa, Tomás
1974 *Plantas medicinales, aromáticas o venenosas de Cuba*. Havana: Academia de Ciencias de Cuba, Ed. Ciencia y Técnica.

Rubio, Angel
1949   *Notas sobre geología de Panamá*. Panama: Imprenta Nacional.
Sahlins, Marshall
1968   "Notes on the Original Affluent Society." In *Man the Hunter*,
          ed. R. B. Lee and I. Devore, pp. 85–89. Chicago: Aldine.
Seemann, Berthold
1854   *The Botany of the Voyage of H.M.S. Herald under Command
          of Captain Henry Kellet, R.N., C.E., during the Years 1845–51.*
          London: Lovell Reeve.
Sherzer, Joel
1983   *Kuna Ways of Speaking: An Ethnographic Perspective*. Austin:
          University of Texas Press.
Sinclair, Françoise G.
1992   "Los amerindios de Panamá en el censo de población de
          1990." *La Prensa* (Panama) 28 April, p. 4B.
Smith, Victoriano
1982   "Los Kunas entre dos sistemas educativos." PhD dissertation,
          University of Siena.
Smythe, Nicholas
1983   *"Dasyprocta punctata and Agouti paca."* In *Costa Rican
          Natural History*, ed. Daniel H. Janzen, pp. 463–465. Chicago:
          University of Chicago Press.
Sousa S., Mario, and Sergio Zárate P.
1983   *Flora mesoamericana. Glosario para Spermatophyta, Español-
          Inglés.* Mexico City: Instituto de Biología, Universidad
          Nacional Autónoma de México.
Sowls, L. K.
1983   *"Tayassu tajacu."* In *Costa Rican Natural History*, ed. Daniel
          H. Janzen, pp. 497–498. Chicago: University of Chicago Press.
Starnes, Wayne; John Lundberg; Karsten Hantel; and Melanie Stassay
1985   "Resultados del estudio de la biota acuática del área del
          Proyecto PEMASKY, Comarca de Kuna Yala." In *Informe de
          la caracterización ecológica del área del Proyecto PEMASKY.*
          Panama: Smithsonian Tropical Research Institute.
Tomlinson, Philip B.
1979   "Systematics and Ecology of the Palmae." *Ann. Rev. Ecol.
          Syst.* 10: 85–107.
Torres de Araúz, Reina
1985   "Etnobotánica Cuna." In *La botánica e historia natural de
          Panamá*, ed. W. G. D'Arcy and M. D. A., pp. 291–298. Correa.
          Saint Louis: Missouri Botanical Garden.
Tosi, J. A., Jr.
1971   *Zonas de vida, una base ecológica para investigaciones
          silvícolas e inventariación forestal en la República de
          Panamá.* Rome: Organización de las Naciones Unidas para la
          Agricultura y la Alimentación.
Tryon, Rolla M., and Alice F. Tryon
1982   *Ferns and Allied Plants with Special Reference to Tropical*

America. New York: Springer Verlag.

Turpana, Arysteides
1982 "La correspondencia del diablo." *Diálogo Social* (Panama) 15, no. 146: 51–56.
1987 *Narraciones populares del país dule*. Mexico City: Editorial Factor.

Uhl, Natalie W., and John Dransfield
1987 *Genera Palmarum. A Classification of Palms based on the Work of Harold E. Moore, Jr.* Lawrence, Kan.: Allen Press

Ventocilla, Jorge
1992 *Cacería y subsistencia en Cangandi, una comunidad de los indígenas kunas*. Hombre y Ambiente, no. 23. Quito: Ediciones Abya Yala.

Wafer, Lionel
1699 *A New Voyage and Description of the Isthmus of America*. London: James Knapton.

Werner, Dagmar, and Daisy Rey
1987 *El manejo de la iguana verde*. Panama: Litografía Enan.

Wilbert, Johannes
1976 "*Manicaria saccifera* and Its Cultural Significance among the Warao Indians of Venezuela." *Botanical Museum Leaflet*, Harvard University 24, no.10: 275–335.
1980 "The Temiche Cap." *Principes* 24, no. 3: 105–109.

Woodson, Schery, et al.
1940– *Flora of Panama*. Annals of Missouri Botanical
1981 Garden. Saint Louis.

Authors

Jorge Ventocilla

Jorge Ventocilla was born in Panama in 1955. He spent his childhood in Peru and returned to Panama to study biology in 1974. Since 1975, he has maintained close ties with the Kuna people.

He has participated in diverse projects focusing on conservation of the environment and the territory of the Comarca Kuna Yala and has worked with the technical planning team of the PEMASKY project, as well as in various environmental education programs. Since 1980 he has worked at the Smithsonian Tropical Research Institute in the Office of Education and Conservation as a specialist on environmental issues. His research interest is the relationship between Kuna culture and wildlife, and subsistence hunting in particular. He has also developed projects in environmental and cultural education for children in conjunction with Kuna artists.

Heraclio Herrera

Heraclio Herrera was born in Ukupseni, Kuna Yala. He studied in Ukupseni and in Panama City and graduated from the University of Panama. He is a biologist specializing in botany. Between 1984 and 1987, as a Smithsonian Fellow, he was a research assistant on the project to inventory the flora of western Kuna Yala, a part of the PEMASKY project. Since 1987 he has participated in several botanical expeditions for the Missouri Botanical Gardens. Herrera has participated in courses and conferences about tropical forests and the ethnobotany of Costa Rica, Panama, Mexico, and the United States. He is committed to the study of plants with cultural and economic significance to the Kuna and to environmental education in Kuna Yala. Since 1992 he has headed the Project for Cultivation and Biological Study of the *ueruk* palm in Kuna Yala.

Valerio Núñez

Valerio Núñez was born in Dad Nakue Dupbir, Kuna Yala. He graduated from the University of Panama with a degree in geography and history. Between 1983 and 1989 he was a member of the PEMASKY planning team and later he was coordinator of its Environmental Education Program. He has participated in a variety of seminars and congresses on environmental protection in Costa Rica, Ecuador, Venezuela, and Bolivia.

For this book, Valerio Núñez recorded the testimony of *caciques generales*, women, educators, and people involved in subsistence activities in Kuna Yala.

Index